I0750132

TRAUMA MADE ME ANGRY.

ANGRY ANGE

GRACE SET ME FREE.

ANGELIQUE FLECKNOE

Ark House Press
arkhousepress.com

All Scripture quotations are taken from multiple versions from the Holy Bible including (NLT) New Living Translation, (KJV) King James Version, (NKJV) New King James Version, (NIV) New International Version and (AMP) Amplified

Unless otherwise stated, all Scriptures are taken from the New International Translation (Holy Bible. Copyright© 1996, 2004, 2007, 2013 by Tyndale House Foundation. Used by permission of Tyndale House Publishers Inc., Carol Stream, Illinois 60188. All rights reserved.)

Some names and identifying details have been changed to protect the privacy of individuals.

Cataloguing in Publication Data:
Title: Angry Ange
ISBN: 978-1-7645620-6-5 (pbk)
Subjects: BIO026000 BIOGRAPHY & AUTOBIOGRAPHY / Memoirs; BIO022000 BIOGRAPHY & AUTOBIOGRAPHY / Women; REL012170 RELIGION / Christian Living / Personal Memoirs.

Design by initiateagency.com

TABLE OF CONTENTS

INTRODUCTION

THE BIRTH OF ANGRY ANGE

My first memory is from about two years of age, growing up in a loving home where you called your parents Grandma and Grandpa; a place where you called your siblings, aunt and uncle. I had four uncles and seven aunts; it was a wonderful life. I lived that happy life till I was about five years of age. At five years of age, an aunt I hadn't met before turned up at my grandma and grandpa's home. I knew she was an aunt because she called my Grandma, Mum and she called my Grandpa, Dad. As a five-year-old, I thought you called your parents Grandma and Grandpa until you were older and then started calling them Mum and Dad; it was what I saw all my other aunts and uncles do. This new aunt told me my Grandparents wanted me to go overseas with her for a one-week holiday, and she told me I would come back to my Grandparents after one week. At five years of age, I didn't understand what a week was. She was persistent that this was what my Grandma and Grandpa wanted. She promised to bring me back in a week so I went with her because no one makes a promise only to break it.

After two years away from my Grandparents at seven years of age, I found out this woman wasn't actually my aunt, she was my birth mother, and she explained how she had reclaimed me as her child and I'd never be going back to my Grandparents. The man and child living with my mother were re-introduced by my mother as my father and brother. I was told to start calling her Mum instead of her real name, like I did with all my other aunts and uncles.

The truth is, I was born out of wedlock by a woman who didn't want me. She tried to hide her pregnancy, and she was grateful she did not show until she was nearly seven months pregnant with me. I was her shame. I was the example of her sinful ways, but when she told me often how she never wanted me, how she just wanted to flush me down the toilet when I was born, I only heard that I was a bad child from birth. When she doted on my younger brother and loved him unconditionally as a child regardless, of whether he was good or bad, I wondered what I had done wrong. When my father started sexually abusing me from eight years of age, I thought it was my own fault. I thought obviously I'd done something wrong for this to start but at eight years of age, I didn't know what I'd done wrong. He'd stand over me and belt me or just sexually abuse me. My mother knew the first time it happened because she was there when I was screaming for help and told her I was dying but she just smiled as though I deserved it. My father told me it was how a father shows love to his daughter; he was doing what dads do to help their daughter to show love. It only happened when I was home alone after that first time. When my mother would slap me and ridicule me for no reason, I hated her but tried to love her because it was the right thing to do. I was always on edge. I started denying my feelings, I'd force myself to become numb until the numbness came naturally.

Food was a trigger for me too. Sometimes my birth mother, who gambled daily, would spend all the money my father earned on her gambling on poker machines. This meant she didn't have money left for food. Many times, when no one was visiting, she would open the fridge and freezer of an evening to cook a meal. If there were a few frozen party pies or a small amount of food she would look at my brother and say that was his dinner not mine. I would have to wait until my father got home at 10pm or 11pm at night as he would get a food voucher from his work for his night shift and would get cakes from the canteen as my dinner. When my father got home, I would be able to select one of the cakes from the assortment to eat as a meal after my brother chose what he wanted for dessert first.

School was one of the places I went to where I could be myself but I didn't know who I was. I tried being the nice Ange, I tried being the mean Ange, I tried being someone other than myself because I didn't know who I was. Because of the way my mother manipulated situations, I ended up being called a liar from primary school, so I stopped denying it and just accepted what others thought about me as true.

I remember turning 13 and my friend at school asked if I'd be having a party. I worked up the courage to ask my mother, and she said it sounded great. She told me we had little money, so I'd have to hand write my invitations. I was so happy I tore blank pages from my schoolbook to write out the invitations. I double checked the date of the party, the theme, how many people I could invite, and my mother confirmed all the details. I wrote a sample of the invite, and my mother said it looked good, so I copied the invite multiple times so I could hand them out at school the next day. I was so excited and happily gave my handwritten invitations out at school to all the girls in my class the following day. My mother told me how she would organize prizes for best dressed and prizes for games. I offered to help but she said not to worry about it because she would organize it for me. I was so happy. She'd never been this kind to me before. Maybe I was getting to an age where she finally accepted me; it was wonderful.

On the morning of my 13th birthday party, I woke to find no present (like normal) but she assured me this afternoon was going to be great, and she'd be busy all day finalising the party because she had a surprise for me. I didn't care about not having a present - I was finally having my first birthday party. The girls at school and I talked about my birthday party during the day and the outfits they'd organized to dress up in for my fancy dress party. When school finished for the day, I felt like skipping home because I was so excited. I don't even remember if I took my little brother home with me that day, maybe I ran ahead; I just remember the feeling of excitement. I ran or skipped the short distance to get home from school.

When I got home to the two-bedroom unit we lived in, it looked just like every other day. No decorations, just nothing. I forced myself to be grateful that my mother had not bothered with decorations because that meant the prizes for games and prize for best outfit would be better. This also meant she had money set aside for party food, I was so excited!! I sat wondering what the surprise would be, I continued to smile about my party. I don't recall my brother being about for my 13th birthday party or maybe he was hiding away in our shared bedroom so he didn't have to be present for the 10 girls I'd invited from my class.

When the first knock happened, my mother smiled and told me to go open the door to let my friends in for my birthday party, as she sat on the lounge. As I opened the door and the first guest arrived, I brought them in, I was so excited. My mother asked what I was doing. I said, "This is my friend, she's here for my birthday party."

My mother said, "Why didn't I know you were having a birthday party, then I could have organized it for you." I was so shocked and I thought to myself, "You told me." At that moment I felt betrayed and in a split second decided to stick up for myself. Then I blurted out, "You said it was okay," but she denied it. Didn't she just say to open the door for my friends for my birthday party?" I thought, how did she all of a sudden forget? I wasn't lying, she was the one who had approved all my handwritten invitations, she was lying, not me. Everyone else arrived while my mother apologized to them denying she even knew about the party, and she was unprepared for anyone to come over. She looked like such a devoted parent, but I had no way to prove my innocence.

Once all the girls from my primary school class turned up, we stood on our small balcony waiting for the hours to pass quickly so they could each escape because who would invite others to their home without telling their parents? I tried explaining that my mother knew about the party but because my mother had called me a liar in front of everyone then everyone else started calling me a liar too. No food or drinks were offered while the 10 girls from my primary school class stood on the balcony with me because my mother said she didn't know about the birthday party. No prizes were given for best dressed, even though all the girls had gone to such a great effort to dress up because my mother explained she had no idea what was going on. All the girls from my class complained how they had spent money buying outfits or how much time they'd spent putting an outfit together. They all looked at me with anger and kept asking why I would lie to all of them but none of them knew it wasn't me lying, it was my mother.

This became a regular thing for my birth mother - saying yes to me then denying it when the day arrived. She never did this to my brother; it was only to me. It created unknown feelings of resentment towards her and everyone else who judged me. I started thinking again how I wasn't good enough and why everyone judged me; maybe they saw I wasn't good enough either and I just had to accept it. No point trying to stick up for myself I thought because no one would believe me anyway.

At around 14 years of age, I started modelling. The modelling agency and brands I worked for asked me to be more myself, but I wondered who that was. I worked for different brands and by year 9 at high school I was absent more than present. Modelling allowed me to walk into a room where other people had been paid to do my make-up, my hair, give me clothes to wear and it was like I was living a fairytale life for those moments. However, going to casting calls and being rejected always hit me as though I was useless and not good enough. My face would get me modelling jobs, but my lack of confidence would sometimes stop the job before it started. I remember how I couldn't be the tutorial model in a collection of videos for a well-known beauty brand because I had no confidence in talking. I couldn't be the model for another well-known company as their brand ambassador because I couldn't be happy while smiling and wearing their clothing line.

To be honest, I wasn't happy, and now I couldn't even pretend to be happy anymore. I was earning money, but the money was used by my mother to pay her bills and continue her gambling addiction. The sexual abuse stopped sometime before modelling started. I didn't realize till later it was because I was at an age where I could become pregnant from the sexual abuse and my parents enjoyed the money they were earning from my modelling jobs over the years. Whether it was $50 for a catwalk job after school at the shopping centre for 20 minutes or $1,000 for a day of photo shoots for brands, my parents kept it all. The extra money I earnt meant my parents, brother and I could move out of the small two-bedroom unit to a rented three-bedroom house.

I started to put on weight and the modelling jobs started drying up. My parents could no longer get money from my modelling, and I was happy and sad about it. Some of the girls at school looked at me differently. I remember walking in the high school yard one day and being stopped by two of the popular girls at school and they showed me a picture from a magazine. As they pointed to it, they asked, "Is that you?" and I said that it was. It was a photo shoot I'd done months earlier for a well-known aerobics and swimwear company. The look on their faces was of disgust. How could

I be a model when I was fat? However, I wasn't going to tell them the truth. I allowed them to ridicule me to a certain degree then I started being nasty to everyone, which only made me unapproachable to most. I talked myself up at times just so no one would find me approachable, then regretted it later when others were mean to me. It was a roller-coaster ride I couldnt get off but I had no one to blame but myself.

I finished high school and was forced into a career. My mother chose my job. I obediently went to the job interview. My parents were happy they had another stable income because as they explained, any money I earnt as their child was to be given to them. My mother never worked unless gambling was a job. I would often think in private how other young people my age were able to go out and party and spend time with friends. If their parents received their week's wage, how did they have money to go out themselves? Maybe they received an allowance; otherwise, how could they go out? I mostly kept to myself at work, trying to please everyone because my life was already so confusing.

After work on Friday night my mother, who was a Seventh Day Adventist, would force me to do Sabbath from Friday night at sunset till Saturday night at sunset. It wasn't all the time but only when there was nothing she planned for us socially. I wasn't allowed to read magazines or watch TV or listen to a radio at that time. I was given a bible and told all I could do is read the bible. I obediently started reading Genesis but couldn't understand it. What was this thing being forced upon me? I didn't get any of it. I'd gone to a Catholic primary school and a Catholic high school. The things they taught were strange and I didn't understand any of that nonsense either.

I remember being thrown out of church in primary school one time because when the whole church was quiet watching the priest, I laughed when the priest got something from a cabinet and said this was the body of Christ. As a child, I wondered how such a small thing from a cabinet on the alter could be someone called Christ and His body. My own birth mother was a religious person when everyone was looking, but a compulsive liar every other time. Who was this God they all prayed to? It all seemed like such rubbish. I didn't agree with any of it, but I had a wonderful Grandpa who talked about his love for God, so I sidelined the whole religious thing and just tried to please everyone. I only had love in my heart for my Grandpa. He had 12 children, but he loved me the most and told everyone I was his favorite. My birth mother hated that her father would say that, about how much he loved me, but she never argued with him in front of me.

Home life was a nightmare. I was still sometimes a servant for my mother, which included her randomly slapping me or making me lie for her. I'd fold washing, clean, and be whatever she needed when no one else, other than my brother and father, were around. She'd use me in whatever way she saw fit because as she explained, I was born to serve her.

This included how my mother would create opportunities for herself to slap me on a regular basis. She'd ask me strange questions that I didn't know the answers to like, "Why aren't you more like your brother?" When she'd ask this question, I'd always look at my brother. He was four years younger than me and he was like a shadow for her; I didn't want to be her shadow, always following her around. They were always together at our home whispering and bossing me around. I didn't want to be like either of them. I'd look at my brother then look at my mother and answer, "I don't know." She'd then slap me for not having an answer and tell me to get to my room. She'd then say, "I don't want to see you for the rest of the night." My mother and brother would then continue sitting on the lounge next to my bedroom and talk loudly about how amazing my brother was.

He was her favorite child. She only had the two of us, but he could do no wrong. She loved him unconditionally. After boasting about her son for long enough, one of them or both of them would knock on the wall to get my attention. I knew this always meant for me to come out of my bedroom. I was useless and didn't even need my name to be called, a knock on the wall was sufficient.

When I came out of my bedroom, she'd scream and ask me why I didn't come out to apologize to her without her telling me I needed to apologize. I could only think at maybe 17, 18 or 19 years of age that she'd clearly said for me to go to my room for the rest of the night because she didn't want to see me. I never understood why I had to apologize for doing nothing wrong. My mother would then slap me again and send me back to my bedroom. After a few minutes of hearing my mother and brother giggling loudly about me being slapped again, I'd then come out to do what she asked and apologize, but it would only incite her to slap me again and tell me, "Didn't I say, to stay in your room for the rest of the night?" It didn't matter if I came out of my bedroom after she said not to come out for the rest of the night to apologize for not being more like my brother. It didn't matter if I ever had an answer prepared on why I wasn't like my brother, instead of saying, "I don't know." She only wanted to slap my face as many times as she could.

I was so confused, but I was certain of one thing; it was fearful to live with my mother. She would know of things I did at primary school because my brother would report to her every afternoon. She also knew of things I'd done when I went to an all-girls Catholic high school until year 10, I never knew how, but she just knew what I'd been up to at school.

In the final two years of high school it was back to being a co-ed school of boys and girls. My mother knew what I was up to because even though my brother was four years younger than me, he was only in the year below me at school (that's what happens when you don't start school until your seven). I was fearful for not lying for her because I'd be slapped again. I was fearful of most things because of her and would lie for her. I would do whatever she said, even if she wasn't around, because I feared getting into trouble all the time. I was sick of being slapped - I was always in the wrong. She was always right. I was just useless, rejected and always wrong.

My mother had groomed my brother to think it was okay to bully others, while my mother and father had groomed me on how to be a victim who was unloved and unworthy. I was everyone's punching bag or tossed around between the two of them being slapped, mentally traumatised, or sexually abused.

I remember my attempt at suicide after high school had finished. I was already working, yet I still felt like a prisoner in my own home. I laid in bed one night and started having these weird thoughts about people cutting their wrists hoping for death as an escape from their own reality. I don't know how the thought started, only that at that moment in time, I was too overwhelmed with sadness; it was like I was in a pit of despair and needed to escape this reality.

I started thinking about how cutting your wrist from left to right or right to left didn't always work and some survived this wrist cutting action. I started thinking about how if I cut up and down on a main vein on my wrist, that would work. I couldn't understand how I knew about suicide all of a sudden as I'd never read about it, but somehow I just knew I couldn't handle another day of this life. I also knew I couldn't get up and go to the kitchen to get a knife while everyone else was asleep, someone would then know what I was up to. So, I just laid in bed, squinted my eyes in the darkness trying to look at my wrist and started scratching along the main vein on the middle, back of my wrist until I scratched the first bit of skin. I thought it would leave a mark if I don't continue finishing this. It stung as I kept scratching with one fingernail along the main vein, but it was my only escape from this living hell.

My thoughts shifted and I started to think about my Grandpa. How would he feel if he heard I'd ended my life? He was already old and I loved him too much to let him hear news of my death, so I stopped scratching and silently cried under the covers because of the pain from my own wrist that I'd caused and also because I knew I wouldn't be able to escape this house of torture tonight.

One day at work, when I was 19 at this time, a colleague invited me to her 21st birthday. I told her I'd have to ask my parents if I could come. She looked at me strangely and asked, "Why?" I explained that's the right thing to do but she still couldn't understand what I was saying. I asked her about her situation to check we were the same. I explained it the same way my mother had explained it to me - we live, we work for our parents, we give all our money to our parents because they gave us life, and we owe them everything. Parents choose what we do every day and every night. Parents choose our friends, etc., and she said, "No!" Our parents give us a life of love. We don't owe them our full wage; we don't owe them every moment of our life. They don't get to make every decision for us because how can we grow as an individual if someone else is making all our life decisions? I thought about what my work friend said and tried to work up the courage to ask my mother about it at some stage. I had to think this through. I never had a way to just talk freely about things at home because everything had to be planned out in my mind first, to make sure I wasn't about to be slapped for bringing up something randomly like my brother always did. I just didn't have the confidence to talk freely at home because I was always on guard to protect myself.

A few days later, my mother advised that one of her younger sisters was coming to stay with us for a few days. She was one of my favorite aunts. I knew my mother would be more reasonable with someone else staying at the house. After dinner, I asked my mother about the 21st birthday party for a friend at work and she just replied, "No!" I asked her why and she said, "You are not allowed to go out to parties or with anyone until you are 21. When you are 21, you will go out with who I tell you to go out with and be back before midnight. You will marry who I tell you to marry. You will do whatever I say." I started to cry and in a split second I thought, is that my life where I get no say in any of it? Through tears I screamed, the first bit of courage I'd ever had about myself at my mother, "No, you're wrong, my friend at work said you don't have the right to demand all my wages. I get to have a say about my life." It all happened so quickly. My mother walked over, slapped my face, grabbed the back of my head and pulled me by my hair, dragging me to the front door. She opened the front door and screamed, "If you can't live by my rules then get out." She then slammed the door behind me. I stood looking at the darkness of neighbor's homes, not knowing what to do. I didn't move off the front doorstep; it was the first time I'd been thrown outside because I'd always been so obedient at home. I heard my aunt asking my mother what she was doing and they started to argue and scream at each other in their own language. Then I heard my aunt say, "Good, if you are throwing her out then throw me out too." At that moment my father appeared. He told my mother and aunt to stop arguing. He opened the front door and told me to get inside and go to my room. We would talk about this tomorrow after work.

That night, I finally made a decision. It was going to be the last night in this house. I was escaping the next day. In those short moments I decided that in the morning I would call my one school friend who knew my mother from primary school to ask for help. If she agreed, then I could escape to her house. If she didn't then I was prepared to be homeless. I left that house that morning thinking to myself, that I never want to return.

My friend said, "Yes!" The first afternoon when staying at my friend's house with her family, my father came over. My friend's parents had called my parents to say I was too scared to come back. My father turned up to my friend's place and explained that my mother had calmed down, and it was ok to go back with him. I said I'd have to think about it but, I was freaking out and told him I needed a few days to think about it. During the week, my aunt who witnessed what had happened the previous night at my parents' home, had already contacted her 10 other siblings to explain what happened. So, when my mother called each of her siblings to say I'd run away, they already knew the truth. My oldest aunt contacted me. She asked what I was going to do. I told her that even though my mother was bad that at least my father was nice to me and I was thinking about going back as I didn't know what else to do. She said, "Don't you know yet?"

I said, "Know what?"

My aunt said, "Your father isn't your real father; he's your stepfather." That day, my relationship with cigarettes was cemented. I must have smoked at least 50 cigarettes a day for the next few days, trying to suppress my emotions with that news. Cigarettes was now my way to suppress emotions.

I distanced myself from most of my family for years after that. The aunts, uncles and cousins I had popped into my life every now and then but I mostly kept my distance from all of them. They'd check in with me to see if I was ok and I told them how wonderful my life was now that I'd escaped that house of torture years before from my mother, stepfather and brother. The one thing I was certain about is I definitely didn't want a relationship of any kind with my mother.

By 24, I had a full-time job as an office all-rounder for a small club in the city. I had a boyfriend who was a successful lawyer. I lived with him and got to drive his convertible brand-new BMW as though it was my own. I attended grand parties, VIP events, ate out all the time at fancy restaurants because he could afford it. I lived in luxury at his apartment on the top floor, which had a 180-degree view from the beach below to the bay. He was successful and I lived a life of luxury because of his success.

My aunts knew where I was because I'd update them when they rang. I didn't make any effort to contact my aunts or uncles because I held offenses to most of them for not helping me when I was living with my mother. They knew this woman had taken me away from my wonderful Grandparents from five years of age but never told me she was my birth mother or warn me not to go with her.

They didn't say anything. At seven years of age a neighbor asked my mother why I hadn't started school yet and she rushed to enrol me into kindergarten at the local state school. They didn't say anything when I called my mother by her first name until another neighbor asked if I was actually my mother's child because they'd seen how she mistreated me. My mother finally told me the truth at seven that she was my birth mother and demanded at that age, I start calling her Mum. They had seen how shy I was but never asked me if I was ok. My aunts and uncles had seen how I never spoke unless someone was talking to me because I was fearful of saying the wrong thing. They had watched as my mother hugged and kissed my brother in front of all of them and openly rejected me. They had watched me from a distance and said they couldn't do anything to help me because they had no way to protect me. They explained it was our islander custom to let the parents take care of the child, they were only aunts and uncles and could only watch my mistreatment from a distance.

The glimmer of hope they saw was only when I was taken by my mother to visit her older sister so I could spend time with my Grandpa. During those visits, all my aunts and uncles would sit and talk and eat with my mother as my brother played with our cousins. I would gladly always sit with my Grandpa in his room talking freely and being hugged and loved by my Grandpa.

One day, while at work, the receptionist rang to say my mother was on the phone. I told her someone was prank calling as I dont have a mother. The receptionist said the woman caller was persistent and suggested I take the call so I could tell the caller myself to explain she was wrong and to stop calling back to bother the receptionist. As the call was put through, it was my mother's voice on the end of the line. "Hello," my mother said and terror ripped through me in an instant, it was her voice.

I bravely said, "What do you want?" She proceeded to tell me how she now had terminal cancer and realized all the wrong she'd done to me in the past and she wanted to apologize to me face to face for all the wrong she'd done to me. She explained how my father also wanted to apologize to me for all the wrong he'd done to me (she's still lying about him being my father I thought). My mother also wanted my brother and me to reconcile before his 21st birthday and asked to meet me. She suggested the place for us to meet. I thought to myself, that it wasn't far from my home, I could walk to meet her. It's a public place. She was no longer in control of my life, I was in control, but I also had this niggling feeling about her intentions. Why now, I wondered after all these years? My mother had never been honest with me before, always manipulating everything. Maybe it was her pending terminal illness. So, I agreed to meet her.

The meeting went as expected, but as my mother spoke, I could tell it was a lie. Her sign that she was about to lie was because her lips started moving. Rarely did she ever talk without a lie. Her words would become more pronounced, her tone always changed when she lied and I knew straight away this was just like all her previous attempts to build me up then make me fall in a heap filled with her lies at my expense. I wondered what she was really up to but pretended like I was there just to listen to her apology, but she didn't apologize.

I finally asked her about her cancer, and she explained about her upcoming operation. The doctors didn't know if it would be successful or not, they only knew if the operation failed, she would be classified as terminal, and she didn't know how much longer she had to live. She gave me her hand and made me feel the small lumps under her skin on her fingers. It was strange holding my mother's hand for the first time in my life, they felt so soft, but I only knew how hard they felt every time her hand had slapped me across my face when I was living with her. The lumps could be moved around; these same moveable lumps were also on her arm. I felt ashamed that I'd thought she was lying about having cancer. You can't fake cancer lumps on your arm but a part of me was relieved that she wasn't lying and yet another part of me was sad at myself for being glad she was about to die a terminal death.

I was relieved when that first visit was over. She explained how she hadn't told my brother about our meeting and he was coming to pick her up soon, so I had to leave before he arrived.

When I got home, I rang an aunt to tell her about what had happened. My aunt said my mother was lying and not to trust her. I told my aunt how my mother got me to feel the lumps on her fingers and her arm and how they moved around under the skin. My mother had explained they were cancer lumps, but my aunt said they weren't, they were fat lumps and not terminal, and that she's lying. Even with that, I decided I'd give my mother the benefit of the doubt. My aunts gossiped and I wasn't sure what to believe.

It was getting close to Christmas when my mother called again to catch up. She said she had a gift for me. I thought to myself, what does one do with giving a gift to a parent that they haven't spoken to in years and that parent is about to die? I decided on a personal gift. I'd give her a Christmas card with the words, 'Merry Christmas Mum, love, your daughter'. Then I'd put $10 in the card. This way I'd see if she was genuine about her apology or fake. If she was genuine then the money was irrelevant as she had a loving card from her daughter, it would have sentimental value. If she was fake in her apology, then she'd be angry about the gift of $10.

I met up with her at the same place as before. It was a family friendly club that offered meals, stage shows but one side of the club was full of poker machines. We didn't get drinks or a meal. She talked about her cancer; how terrible everything was. I asked her who my birth father was and the lies started from her lips. She changed the subject, and handed me a large package and asked me to unwrap it. It was an oversized black and white jumper that I had no use for, but I politely thanked here. She asked if I had anything for her and I handed her the envelope I'd prepared.

My mother smiled a wide smile then opened the envelope and looked at me in disbelief. She sat opposite me and started screaming at me in the family friendly club for all to hear her anguish, "Why only $10?" she said. "I know you live in that penthouse," as she pointed to it," and you drive a convertible BMW. I tell you I'm dying of cancer and you give me $10." The truth had been revealed as she discarded the card, and held the $10 tightly between her finger and thumb. My aunts knew I didn't want to have anything to do with my mother, stepfather or brother yet they couldn't stop their evil tongues from gossiping about me to her. My mother knew I was doing well because of unnecessary updates from her siblings and wanted to take what was mine for herself. She was only after money, not to repair a relationship between mother and daughter. I pulled out the packet of cigarettes from my jacket pocket at that moment. My mother looked in disbelief.

"What is that?" She asked.

I replied, "They're called cigarettes."

She said, "If you're having that I'm not staying."

"No one's keeping you here," I said, as I stared directly at her. She got up in a huff and walked away with her $10 note.

I watched her walk towards the poker machines. "No one will ever mistreat me again," I thought, and at that moment, Angry Ange was born.

CHAPTER 1

PRIDE CAME IN UNANNOUNCED

A SHORT SERIES OF RANDOM ANGRY ANGE STORIES

Getting Baguettes But Sending The Bird

One day, I needed baguette rolls for a lunch I was preparing. The shop was walking distance from my home that I lived in with my lawyer boyfriend. Life was amazing. I wasn't married, no children but living the high life seemed grand.

I decided that instead of walking the two minutes I'd instead drive my boyfriend's brand-new convertible BMW down to the shops because I felt lazy and needed to reserve my energy for socialising with friends who were coming over to visit.

As I purchased my baguettes, I noticed two girls looking at me. I instantly recognized them as the two girls who used to bully me in kindergarten when I first started school at age seven at a state school. They used to call me a freak because I didn't know how to speak English.

I wondered why they were so mean to me back then. I wondered in that moment why they always thought they were better than me. Could they not see that as a child I was already having so many problems at home?

However, they never asked when I was little and now, they started the same tactics they did when we were all in kindergarten. They pointed at me, sniggered to each other and started to laugh, thinking they were still better than me.

I stood behind my BMW, without looking away from them, and I pressed a button on the car remote. The roof opened on the car and tucked itself away in the boot to show it was a convertible. They stood looking at me without blinking, possibly wondering if I was the same girl they bullied back in kindergarten and I smiled. I gestured with my third finger up in the air to them, then hopped into my car and drove off as their mouths remained open in shock. "I was better than them," I thought, as I drove the two minutes to get home.

Bus Ride - Why Are Dogs On A Bus?

One Friday night after the night club closed, my two girl friends and I decided to get the bus home from our girls' night out. The bus would only take 20 minutes. None of us girls were too drunk to the point we couldn't walk but we were all over the legal driving limit. The three of us paid our fairs and found our seats. My friends sat at the front seats closest to the driver, while I sat a few rows behind them. Five other people were on the bus that night, the rest of the 30-seater bus was empty.

A beautiful islander girl sat in the chair to my right with her male friends. I looked at her and remember thinking how lucky she was to have four protective brothers with her so late at night. She saw me looking and as I looked away, I leaned forward and put both my hands on my knees. I was wearing a tiny bra top and leather pants, but my mid drift was exposed. She said, "You're fat." I looked at her wondering if she was talking to me and she smiled as she stared straight at me and pointed at my stomach. I looked down to notice one line across my flat stomach as I bent over, I wasn't fat at all. How dare she insult me.

I looked at her and asked, "Are you talking to me?"

She said, "Yes, you're too fat to wear that outfit."

I instantly snapped back, "With a face like yours, get back to the pound, you dog." She had a look of frustration on her face. Anyone else would have just said nothing because she had four large male friends with her who looked intimidating - but not me. She was messing with the wrong person. I was also an islander so she didn't scare me and neither did her four male friends. I proceeded to verbally abuse her for the rest of the ride home.

The male friends she was with all looked at me, they must have been thinking, "Is that girl for real or just stupid?" I told her to just try saying anything else and I'd fight her in front of her male friends. Her male friends had done nothing wrong to me, but I asked her if she needed me to wipe that smug smile off her face. She went silent. The next stop was my stop. My two girlfriends who'd lost their voice the entire trip because of this exchange screamed out to the girl seated to my right, "Go back to the pound," as they quickly exited the bus, not wanting to be harmed. They were more sensible than me because they feared retribution, but not me. I was facing every bit of ridicule head on these days. No one would ever disrespect me again. As I got up from my seat, I looked at the girl and her four male friends who were still seated on the bus. I stood in front of them then told her if she ever appeared in front of me again that I'd hit her and I walked off the bus to join my friends.

That same weekend, on Sunday night, I went with other night clubbing friends to a different club. This club was a place all the young locals went to on a Sunday night. The place had a large dancefloor area and a long bar.

Outside was a balcony that stretched the length of the club, and it overlooked the beachfront.

As I walked into the room, I looked around for any of our other friends, and I saw that same girl from the bus on the dance floor. I walked towards her, wanting to walk straight past her, so she could see how wonderful I looked. I stood tall, pulled my shoulders back and wanted to prove to her I wasn't fat like she'd said on the bus two nights earlier. She didn't have any of her male friends with her. She saw me and started whispering to her girlfriends about me. She started pointing at me and laughing. How dare she! I walked straight up to her instead of walking past her. I threw her to the ground and told her to never look in my direction again, then I walked off. How dare she be so disrespectful to me I thought as I found our other friends and enjoyed another night of drinking and dancing.

Getting Take Out But Delivering Instructions

Finding my prince charming and having children was a dream come true. We'd met through mutual friends and found we had so many chances in the past to meet but the timing never seemed right. I'd broken up with my lawyer boyfriend, and he had broken up with his long-term girlfriend. It was like all the stars aligned when we finally met. We had children together and every opportunity to spoil them, and we did it.

Picking the kids up from primary school, they'd always ask for take away. It was either KFC or McDonald's. This particular day the kids chose McDonald's. I drove through the drive-through with the kids in the car. As I approached the first window I asked for two happy meals and paid. I drove to the second window to collect my order but as I pulled up, I saw the young store manager talking and laughing with friends to the side of the cash register. I thought to myself that they weren't customers, they were socialising and totally disregarding me as an important customer. The young man looked at me in the drive-through, came to the window and demanded I go around to the front waiting bay for my order.

Before I could say anything he abruptly closed the little window in the drive through and walked off to continue talking and laughing with his friends. In that moment, I decided he doesn't have the right to disrespect me, I'm a paying customer. Without a customer, he didn't have a job. He needed to do his job instead of socializing, so I decided to stay put and not move my car to the waiting bay. I was in a hurry and how dare he just socialize while I was in a hurry.

Minutes went by, then a staff member inside the store yelled out to ask why the driveway was backed up and the manager looked at me and came up to the window in a rage. He screamed, "I told you to go round the front."

I screamed back "Get my food instead of socializing on work time. I'm watching you so don't dare spit in my food." I got the happy meals and passed them to my children. I thought to myself, that my kids will see how brave their Mum is and always stick up for them. However, in reality, they were so embarrassed that they no longer wanted McDonald's, but I was too prideful to notice their embarrassment.

We started stopping at KFC instead of McDonald's as an after-school treat for the kids because I was angry with that young McDonald's store manager and I wanted him to know that he'd missed out on an important customer because of his rudeness to me. But because I was also rude to KFC staff, they started telling me they'd run out of chicken and couldn't serve me. How does a chicken shop like KFC run out of chicken? I never realized at the time that I'd been secretly blacklisted from my local McDonald's and KFC. Going through the staff entrance to demand why the food was taking too long as I sat in the waiting bay of these drive-throughs seemed like a normal thing anyone would do.

Getting Pizza But Being Blacklisted

My husband and I went to visit one of his childhood friends. We drove the eight hours to their home and were greeted by my husband's friend, his beautiful wife and their three adorable children. Our kids loved visiting them too. We weren't related by blood but they were family we chose for ourselves. After a few days of home cooked meals, we decided that the wives should have a night off from cooking and order pizza to be home delivered. Everyone ordered their favourite pizzas and the adults sat and chatted whilst the kids played.

The pizza was delayed and I wanted to ring the local pizza store to ask about the delay but held off as we were at our friends' place and they said the pizza was good, so we all continued to wait. The kids became restless as they were now all starving. When is this pizza going to arrive, I thought. It had been nearly two hours since the pizza order was made. Then a knock was heard at the door. The pizzas had finally arrived, all the kids became excited, and everyone else was glad the food had arrived, but I was irritated on why it took so long. The delivery man didn't apologize for the delay and just shoved the pizzas at us and left. There was no point waiting for a tip, I thought. What a lousy delivery driver taking so long to drive what should have been 10 minutes from his store to our friends' place but it took him nearly two hours. My friend always had a kind heart and was prepared to give him a tip; she's very sweet but the driver had already gone. Good riddance to him! The driver shoved the pizza boxes at us then walked off in a huff back to his car.

The kids all came with their plates to grab a few slices of pizza. I brushed off my annoyance of the delivery driver and looked forward to us all having pizza together. As each piece was taken from the delivery box, the ingredients on the pizzas started sliding off each slice. The sauce base was so watery that the toppings slid straight off each pizza slice. Had they even been cooked properly? I looked at the number of uneatable pizzas and thought about the money we spent on them and felt like I needed to fix the situation. The kids ate; they were starving but none of the adults could eat the pizzas. The adults, though, were not happy. They just talked about their disappointment of the pizzas with each other but not me. "That's it," I thought, I couldn't handle another moment of this injustice. "I'm going to call them and ask for an explanation," I announced.

Our friends started laughing and said, "Don't worry, we can't wait another two hours for them to fix and deliver more pizzas," but I'd stopped listening. I was going to fix this situation for all of us. I went to our friends' landline phone, picked up the receiver and dialled the pizza place. I proceeded to tell the pizza store manager of my disgust with his pizzas, that he should be ashamed of himself, and why two hours for watery, cold pizza, etc? He ended up apologizing over the phone. He didn't realise it was that bad but would remake our pizzas free of charge and promised they would all be delivered within half an hour. He asked for the other pizzas to be given back to him.

Exactly 30 minutes later there was a knock on the door; new pizzas had been delivered by the same delivery driver as before. I collected the new pizzas and shoved the cold, watery pizzas at the delivery driver then slammed the door in his face. The new pizzas were great and really tasty. I thought, "Why weren't they made like this the first time?" I was proud of myself for sticking up for everyone after we left our friends to drive the eight hours back home. A few weeks later, we found out that the pizza place, which was the only pizza place in town, now refused to deliver pizzas to our friends' home. It became difficult when our friends wanted pizza delivered after that, as they had been blacklisted by the pizza place because of my rudeness. In the end the only way they could get pizza delivered to their home was to order pizzas under a different name and they pretended they were new homeowners who had just moved in. No, they told the pizza shop, no angry islander lady lived at their address.

Mafia, Knock And Run

I have a cousin who was a mischief maker as a child. We'd lost contact as we grew up. One day, 20 years after we last spoke, my cousin called me out of the blue. He was moving interstate, not far from my home. After 20 years apart, we'd now live 15 minutes away from each other. I didn't have any family from my side who lived nearby so it was lovely. He came to our home with his wife and three daughters (the eldest was 15, his middle child was 10 and his baby daughter was two years old). Our children now had cousins from both their mother and father, the more family for the kids - the more the merrier.

The first few weeks were amazing, spending time with my little cousin and his family made me so happy. Our daughter only had male cousins on her father's side, she loved them like brothers, but these were girl cousins who she could play makeup with, do dance competitions with. They were like sisters for her and she loved them instantly.

As weeks turned into months, my little cousin and his family became regular visitors at our home, and our daughter loved visiting them too. They treated her with surprises that we couldn't afford like front row tickets to my daughter's singing idol. He was only a teenager too at the time and she wore his t-shirts, had his books, played his music and talked constantly about how she loved Justin Beiber, just like every other teenage girl at that time. My cousin and his wife had bought their daughters tickets and gifted my daughter the same, which included front row tickets to a sold-out Justin Bieber concert. They were staying at the same hotel as Justin Beiber. My cousin had spared no expense. I told him, I couldn't afford the gift he'd given my daughter, but he said, "Don't worry cuz; she's like a daughter to us too." They were family. There was no need to worry. My husband didn't like the gift, it was too extravagent, but I ignored him every time he brought it up. He didn't understand that my little cousin was just doing things for us out of love because my cousin had no ulterior motive.

As more months passed, my cousin introduced me to some of his friends, I was always polite, but something seemed off. They were his business associates; they either talked briefly or didn't say a word. When I said, "Hello," they'd just smile and nod but we had no conversations as we all ate meals together.

My cousin started telling me his problems. I was his closest family member, and he trusted me so much to be his confidant about our relatives that had disappointed him since his Mum (my eldest aunt) had died. He shared his grievances of how some of our relatives were using him for his money; they were gossiping and making up lies amongst each other about him, all because of his success. I thought how I hadn't noticed our relatives using or lying to me before. When I had my own little family, our relatives popped in for overnight visits to say, "Hello," and share a meal. They weren't there to harm any of us. They did bring treats or surprises for the kids. Everyone in my family was doing things out of love for each other but now I built my guard up about my own relatives. How dare they cause such problems for my little cousin who had done nothing wrong. So I started talking back to my relatives, questioning them on why they were being so nice to me, questioning them on why they were being so disrespectful to my little cousin but they all denied it. What liars they were as I started to distance myself from relatives and draw closer to my little cousin and his family. My little cousin needed me, and I was going to protect him. I cut off relationships with relatives to stick up for my little cousin.

More months passed and my cousin and his wife started telling me of things they'd noticed about my husband's side of the family. Things they heard them whisper about my husband, my children and me, while I wasn't in the room. I thought it was wonderful to have someone who cared about me that much to always be honest with me even if it meant gossiping about others. The negative commentary about my husband's family continued from my cousin and his wife until, one day I sat and thought how I'd now lost some of my closest relatives - I'd deliberately cut ties with them as I stuck up for my little cousin. We'd never had a problem before but now I'd severed all ties with them.

My husband's family had never done anything wrong to me but why now were we starting to have problems? I loved them just like I loved the family I'd severed relationships with. I wondered whether my little cousin and his family were deliberately sowing discord. I spent time sitting in silence some days just thinking about it all. What's going on? I wish I knew the truth!

Later that week my phone rang, but I missed the call because I was busy preparing dinner for my husband and children. My phone beeped that a voicemail message was received. I looked and saw the message was from my cousin's wife; it was at least three minutes long. "I'll listen to it later," I thought. If it was urgent, she'd call back.

After my children were put to bed, I grabbed my phone and cigarettes and I went outside to listen to the lengthy voicemail. The message was of a conversation between my cousin and his wife. Their baby daughter who was playing with her Mum's phone, had dialled me accidentally. She did not know the call went to my voicemail as she sat playing on her Mum's phone while she sat in the same room as her parents. The voicemail was of my cousin, his wife and another person who was on speaker phone. It was so wrong to be listening to their conversation, but it was about how the police had conducted a raid. I loved watching Law and Order and felt like I was one of the detectives listening in on a call for clues. The voicemail continued, the police were everywhere and they were lucky not to be caught. "Be careful," they said to each other as they talked quickly. They talked about how shots were fired but no one was killed. I quickly hung up on the voicemail then deleted it. I wasn't interested in hearing anything else they talked about. So strange, I thought. I'd only just been wondering about the truth and now this message. I wondered if it was a sign to distance myself from my cousin. The damage to my own relatives had been done; it could not be salvaged as too much time had now passed.

The next time my cousin rang and started making negative comments about my husband's family, I questioned him about it. "Why are you doing this and sowing such discord, are you trying to make me severe all ties with everyone else we know as family but you?"

He said, "No!" but I somehow saw through his lie for the first time. I started questioning him about what businesses he actually had - his answer was another lie. I felt so foolish. I'd grown up with a birth mother who was a compulsive liar and yet I didn't realize my own cousin, my little cousin, was just the same. He was also a compulsive liar who manipulated situations for his best interest. I severed ties with my cousin in that phone call. I wasn't allowing him to cause any more pain to others I cared about. I was not going to lose any more family who I cared about.

I cried that night because of the family I'd loved but lost, but it was my own fault. I tried calling each of them back at least 20 times, one call after another. It was just like they'd done to me so many months earlier when they were searching for reasons why I'd treated them the way I did. The nasty posts I did on their social media accounts, and the horrible messages I sent them in anger about how they could say such terrible things about my children. At the time I was so angry and reflected on how dare they do this, but now I realized it wasn't them that was the problem, it was me for believing in lies. I'd been deceived by someone I trusted. I passed hurt to family not knowing the pain I'd caused. The decades of love between other family members and me deserved a conversation at the time but I was too enraged to see the truth. Now that I knew the truth, it was too late.

More months passed and I realized just how much time my cousin and his family had intertwined with mine, so much free time. I was still angry about how it all happened but not angry at my little cousin and his family. I was angry with myself for being so foolish. I'd treated pearls as trash and trash as pearls.

One afternoon, as my husband, children and I were watching a kid's movie together, someone started knocking loudly at my front door demanding I open the door. I opened the door to see one of my cousin's friends standing there. What now? He started yelling at me to tell him where my cousin was. How would I know? I hadn't seen him in months. As my little cousin's friend continued to shout at me to tell him where my cousin was, I started remembering gossip I'd overheard about my cousin from my aunts. His businesses were not legal; they'd asked me to keep my distance from my little cousin, yet they wanted to spend time with him themselves. It all sounded so hypocritical.

I'd been told at the time to stop talking to my little cousin but I shrugged the words off as more gossip from family. Why tell such lies? I wondered as I ignored them. But suddenly. I remembered they said he had been interacting with mafia characters and drug dealers. I'd originally shrugged this off as lies at the time. I didn't even know if the man screaming and pointing his finger at me was from the mafia with his thick European accent. I didn't even know this man's name. I only knew I'd seen him before with my cousin on multiple occasions; he was supposed to be my cousin's friend.

He asked me questions and I answered, "I don't know." I thought about my family inside. Would this man barge in, to hurt my family? I thought that he wouldn't. Suddenly replying, "I don't know," triggered past trauma in me, like when my birth mother used to ask me ridiculous questions I'd never know the answers to, and it was always followed by a slap from her. Something inside me snapped. This is my turf; he was on my front yard, not some public place. He had no idea that he'd just knocked on the one door of the wrong person. Instead of shying away from his barrage of questions I now walked out of my front door towards him. I started shouting at him, and I started pointing my finger at him.

He started walking backwards, possibly wondering to himself who this lunatic was but I hadn't finished with him. The look in his eyes said that this woman is crazy. He thought she looked like she was about to attack him with her raised voice and angry demeanour. He realized to himself that I wasn't worth it. I knew nothing because I'd already cut ties with my cousin some months before. I wasn't my cousin's keeper. "Get out," I screamed at the man who I was ready to have a fist fight with. He turned and walked back to his car. I was still screaming at him as he drove off. How dare anyone come to my home and treat me like that. Luckily, I could be strong for my family and me. I never saw my cousin's friend again.

It's My Way Or It's My Way

Everyone knew I was in charge. I wasn't some elusive CEO; I wasn't even a manager, but I controlled every narrative and situation. I was no one's pushover because I didn't like most people but the ones I did like, it was my job to protect them. Whether it was my children, my family, my friends or my work friends, they all got the same choices. I'd say, "Here are your options, it's my way or it's my way."

I was a total control freak. Everything at home had to be a certain way. Every catch up with friends meant I scrutinised everything about new people who were invited to these gatherings. The same with work. If I liked you, I'd have a conversation with you because I felt safe but if anyone didn't meet my standards, they were out of my circle of friends before they had a chance to say hello. In some cases, it was even if they looked at me the wrong way and I'd think to myself that you're out before your even in, then I'd smile and walk away. I had a small circle of friends but the friends I had; I loved deeply. You just can't like some people. I didn't like everyone and I had a specific reason for not liking them and I made sure they knew about it.

A lady I worked with at a manufacturing business tried to speak to me one day; she was our Production Manager. I liked her at first but after some years I found her annoying. She'd been caught lying to my friends at work but all of them kept smiling and talking with her. I would think to myself, "Why don't they just tell her to go away?" I couldn't understand why people sat on a fence about right and wrong. These people smiled at you to your face then talked about you behind your back. No one ever thought I was a fence sitter because it was either right or wrong and, in most cases, I was right and everyone else was wrong!

The Production Manager came up to me at work one day and tried to have a conversation. She said, hello. "Goodness gracious," I thought to myself in an instant, "had I not made myself clear that I didn't like her?" In my mind all I could think of was that you're out, but my mouth and actions were abrupt because I didn't care how she felt. I stretched out my hand to grab my cigarettes from my desk to go out to the smoker's area looked at her and said, "Stop speaking to me. Don't you know everything you say is like verbal diarrhea?" Then I smiled and walked off. I didn't care what others thought; you just can't like some people, and I knew the truth about her, and I was taking a firm stance for my truths.

A few weeks went by at work, and everything this woman did was annoying to me. She'd started with a lie at first and then would make more lies to cover her original lie. She reminded me of my birth mother. She also made my other friends at work, her own production staff, stand and wait till she was ready - she did it all the time.

One day I looked at her from my desk - she was on her social media. The Production Supervisor came to ask her about what was next and she told them to wait while she finished something important. I looked and saw her finishing a post on her personal social media account as the Production Supervisor just stood there waiting. After a few minutes I got up from my own desk, walked over to the Production Manager's desk, smiled at the Production Supervisor with a look that quietly said, "I'll stand up for you," and slammed my hand on the Production Manager's desk, and yelled, "Hurry up, get off your social media and do your job. Staff are waiting for your update at work not your social media." She looked away from her mobile phone and without looking at her computer gave the Production Supervisor the update. How dare she! Why couldn't she just give that production update five minutes ago?

This Production Manager continued to annoy me. I looked around the office, and wondered why anyone else hadn't said anything for the Production Supervisor. I shrugged it off; I had taken care of the situation, then I grabbed my cigarettes and walked out to the smoker's area.

Another week went by and the owners of the manufacturing business I worked for were coming in for a visit. They lived interstate and came up every month. They had another production factory in another state and travelled between the two sites. They were a dynamic husband and wife duo who owned this family manufacturing business. They were both the owners, but we always took instructions from the husband; he was in charge, and he was our Managing Director. His wife took the title of Marketing Manager, but we all knew she was also one of the owners. She came into work with her husband but had her own business; it wasn't manufacturing, but this job title just meant she could travel with her husband. She did do a lot of great work on advising us with advertising flyers, but she didn't produce the flyers, she just gave guidance on them. I loved how much they cared about each other. The wife would bring cut up vegetables and fruit for her husband and put them on his desk always checking in on him to make sure he ate whatever she brought to him. He would always smile and munch on the healthy snacks she brought him throughout the day.

As I walked into work one morning, the owner's wife, our Marketing Manager, waved to me from her office. "Good morning," I said as she gestured for me to come in, close her office door and sit with her. I put my laptop bag down in the empty chair next to where I sat, opposite her, at her desk and smiled. She said, "The Production Manager has spoken with my husband and me. She feels you don't like her. Is that right?" I wondered, how that silly Production Manager could think I don't like her. Why wasn't she sure I totally disliked her?

I nodded, "It's true," I said.

"What do you mean?" asked our Marketing Manager.

"It's true, I don't like her. I have no time for her," I replied.

Our Marketing Manager looked at me and said, "Angie, can you please try to be friends with her."

I shook my head and said, "No, I can't. She's rude to her own staff, she lies and I don't want to be her friend."

The Marketing Manager went silent. She looked at my crossed arms with a firm look of defiance on my face and asked, "Is there no grey area with you?"

I knew what she meant but I shook my head again and said, "No, it's black, or it's white, it's right, or it's wrong; there is no grey area! I can't be friends with a liar."

Our Marketing Manager softened her gaze and asked, "Could you at least have a conversation with her? Please do it for my husband and me," she asked.

I thought for a moment and said, "Okay," I nodded. "I can talk to her, but I won't be friends with her; she's a liar."

Our Marketing Manager, smiled. "Okay," she said, "as long as you say hello and not ignore her."

I nodded and thought to myself, "Yes, I can do that."

I left the Marketing Manager's office and I looked at the Production Manager's desk. I had to walk past her to get to my own desk. She looked up and smiled at me like a cheshire cat who had just caught the one thing it had been trying to catch. She had me in her grasp, and I had no way to ignore her today like I normally did.

As I went to walked past her, she put her mobile phone down, rested her elbows on her desk and said, "Hello Angie." I looked at her with disgust and thought how dare she instigate the conversation now. I wasn't ready, so I just smiled; it was a fake smile but passable.

I said, "Hello."

She asked, "How are you?" but I could see straight through her tactic, of course, she knew how I was. She had dobbed me into the owners for ignoring her, for disliking her and for not wanting to be friends with her. She didn't understand that the reason I did it was because she always lied so I thought, I'll make it clear.

I smiled a genuine smile at our Production Manager and asked, "Have you heard that new Meaghan Trainor song?"

She shook her head and said, "No, what is it called?"

I said, "I can't remember the full name but the words are, 'You open up your mouth, and you lie, lie, lie.' I heard someone else in the office giggle. The Production Manager didn't know what to say and she just sat looking at me with shock.

I walked past her and put my laptop bag on my desk. I grabbed my cigarettes and proceeded to walk out to the smokers' areas - so proud of myself! I'd done what the owners wanted. I hadn't lied to them, I'd acknowledged her and spoken to our Production Manager today instead of ignoring her like I normally did, but like every other time I agreed to do something, it was done my way or my way.

CHAPTER 2

TAKING CONTROL - I'M IN CHARGE

A SHORT SERIES OF RANDOM ANGRY ANGE STORIES

The Mother Of Disappointment

It had been a normal day at work, nothing out of the ordinary, yet that night when I went to bed I couldn't stop thinking of my Grandpa. I hadn't seen Grandpa in a few months. During those absent months I'd been overseas with my lawyer boyfriend. He flew me first class through Europe, and we stayed at exclusive hotels, but when we came back, we decided we weren't a good match for each other, so I moved out of his penthouse apartment, and we amicably went our separate ways. I realized during the trip, that money can't buy you happiness. Another few months went past after the breakup, and I was enjoying being single for the first time in many years.

The next morning when I woke up, I kept thinking about my Grandpa. I went to work as normal and contacted a younger aunt about him. She said she'd been to visit him that morning. She did that often and he was fine, so I sighed with relief and kept doing my work. By lunch time the thoughts of my Grandpa kept coming back to mind. I asked the elderly lady I worked with, what I should do, and she said you're missing him, just go and see him. I had no way to get to my Grandpa; he lived with an older aunt and the only way I could see him was if I hired a car for myself to drive to her home. I rang the car rental company, and they confirmed they had a car available for collection at 5pm. I planned to catch the train to the car rental place then drive directly to my Grandpa for a catch up.

This was a Tuesday afternoon at 5pm when everyone was clocking off work to head home. The hire car had been finalized, and I sat in traffic waiting for the lights to turn from red to green, so I could start the drive to see Grandpa. Suddenly, my heart started beating extra fast, my head became dizzy, and I started to panic, but I didn't know what was happening to me. I instantly thought of my Grandpa and rang my older aunt who my Grandpa lived with. My older aunt's husband answered the phone. I asked him if I could speak to Grandpa and he said that I couldn't. I asked why and he said because he's gone. I wondered why my Grandpa would go out. He was in a wheelchair these days, so I asked this uncle who took my Grandpa out, and he replied, "He's dead." I asked to speak with his wife, and my older aunt came on the phone; she was crying.

I asked her if it was true and she said, "Yes," The people from the morgue were on their way.

I said, "You've never done me a favor before but please just do this one favor. Please don't let the people from the morgue take Grandpa until after I've arrived and said goodbye to him." She agreed. I drove home, changed into a new outfit I'd bought from Italy from my European holiday to go and say goodbye to my Grandpa.

I drove from my home to my Grandpa's home in 20 minutes. It should have taken 40 minutes, but I felt like I no longer had any reason to live and drove more than double the speed limit to arrive before the people from the morgue took my Grandpa away. As I drove, I screamed abuse to the God my Grandpa believed in and asked, "Why did you take my grandpa away?" He was only 93 years old. I had nothing now that my Grandpa was gone.

I arrived and parked the car and noticed all my family (aunts, uncles and cousins) all standing huddled together out the front of the house at the top of the driveway, next to where the funeral car was parked. I was shocked, and wondered how they all knew to be here and why hadn't anyone told me? My favorite aunt came up to me and said, "Hello," and all I could think of was why didn't YOU call me? I just stared at her blankly for a moment while frustration, anger and rage built up inside me. My entire family - over 50 of them were here already; some would have travelled for over an hour to be here. However, not one person thought to ring me to tell me my Grandpa was unwell. So, I could still see him while he was alive. They'd all said their goodbyes but not one of them had thought of me. I thought to myself, "What a bunch of losers," While my Grandpa was alive, he was very open and told everyone that even though he had 12 children and many grandchildren, I was his favorite. Had they deliberately avoided telling me the truth, so they didn't have to hear their own father tell me before his last breath, something they didn't want to hear? How dare any of them think after today we could be family. My anger and rage came to a boiling point, but I quickly looked away from them.

As I started to walk along the long driveway I thought about my wonderful Grandpa. I could see the room ahead where my Grandpa was in; it was past the front door of the main house towards the separate dwelling at the top of the driveway. The funeral car was parked just outside the room my Grandpa was in and on the grass area to the right is where the rest of my aunts, uncles and cousins all stood. I needed to say my own goodbye to Grandpa.

"Get out of here," I heard someone to my left scream and as I turned my head to look who it was, it was my birth mother.

"What did you say?" I asked her with a stern voice.

She repeated herself, "Get out of here, no one wants you here." I looked at my so-called family standing a short distance away then back to my birth mother.

"He's my grandpa, I've come to say goodbye."

My mother yelled at me again, "He's my father not yours. I'm your mother and I said get out." In that moment, I couldn't believe all my family, was just standing there silently. Who was going to be here for me now that my Grandpa had died?

I looked at my birth mother and said, "Do not tell me what to do. You don't have the right to be a parent to me now. Even a dog owner needs to get a licence. You're not fit to be a parent. You are only disappointment." I started walking closer to my birth mother as I pointed at her face, no longer the scared child I once was. "I'm going to go and say goodbye to my Grandpa and when I'm finished, I'm coming back to deal with you!" Everyone around me continued to stay silent, and no one moved as I walked from the end of the driveway into the room where my Grandpa was laying.

I saw his lifeless body on the bed. He looked like he was asleep. I grabbed my Grandpa's hand and willed for him to wake up but he didn't wake up. I cried, telling him how sorry I was that I was late. I cried tears of regret, tears of sadness and as I held his hand talking to him, I felt a tap on my shoulder. It was one of the men from the funeral home telling me they had to take my Grandpa away. I kissed and hugged my Grandpa goodbye and walked out of his room.

I walked silently towards the end of the driveway away from the house and stood on a separate grass area at the bottom of the driveway, away from all my so-called family who continued to stand in front of the funeral car at the opposite end of the driveway. I turned my back on all my family and closed my eyes as I waited in silence for the funeral car to leave. I was paying my last respects to my wonderful Grandpa through moments of silence as my broken heart grieved for him. I heard the hearse door close. I heard the funeral car drive past me. I continued to stand in silence with my eyes closed as I imagined the funeral car turn out of my older aunt's street. I imagined as it left her street and drove onto the main road. I turned to look at my family.

I opened my eyes and looked with disgust at my so-called family then screamed, "Where is she?" After all those years of torment, all those years of being a boxing bag for my birth mother and someone her husband stood over to sexually abuse. My anger was at its peak, the time had come for retribution, and no one was standing in my way. A family member told me my mother had locked herself in the house as she was scared of me. Apparently, she had called her husband and son to come rescue her because I'd gone crazy. So, I screamed at her from the front yard as she hid in the house, "Get out here you coward. Today I plan on dealing with you, your husband and your son in front of all our family so they can see the real you and you can no longer lie about everything." However, the front door had been locked, and no one was forcing her out of the house.

One of my aunts came to me but I brushed her away in disgust while I thought about how dare you all stick up for that woman inside. What kind of family are you? My so-called aunt had contacted my ex-boyfriend and asked him to persuade me to leave. She knew we'd already broken up but she didn't want a scene as we were all grieving in that moment. It was better if I just went home so they could all grieve together.

I left like an obedient niece waiting to hear about the funeral arrangements from my aunts and uncles in the coming days. I went home and spent the next few days crying. I went to see a doctor about my grief. I needed some form of happy pill, but the doctor said that because I hadn't slept in days instead he suggested I take half a sleeping tablet, but I wanted to think about my Grandpa. I didn't want to spend a moment asleep. I didn't want to spend another moment without thinking about my Grandpa. What good was me resting when he was now dead?

After days of not sleeping and just crying, I pulled myself together knowing that my Grandpa's funeral would be overseas so he could be buried next to my Grandma in their burial tomb. I checked the available limit on my credit card. It was enough to fly back for my Grandpa's funeral. After another couple of days, I contacted my older aunt where my Grandpa had lived. I hadn't heard from any of my aunts or uncles with any update of funeral arrangements. The call was answered. I was told my aunts and uncles had a family meeting and out of respect for my mother I wasn't allowed to go to the funeral. If I didn't listen and went anyway then they would make sure I was totally excluded and it would be better for me if I didn't come at all. I pleaded with them to let me go, I cried and begged but without any emotion, they just said "No." I wiped my feet from my family after that conversation.

They knew what I'd been through as a child. They lived through the lies my birth mother told, yet they were all oblivious to my pain. Not one of them called me before the funeral. One aunt, out of guilt, brought me a gift back from our island homeland in the South Pacific where my Grandpa had been buried. She bought it as a gift for me after my Grandpa's funeral to show me she had been thinking of me, but I threw it back at her. "What good is this handbag?" I said. "Can it bring me any memories of my Grandpa's funeral? Can it give me time to spend with Grandpa, like you all had before he took his last breath? No, it can't," I screamed. I'd had enough with my family, they didn't want me, and now I made a choice - I didn't want them either.

I wondered for weeks what my Grandpa would have said to me if I'd turned up to see him before his death. I wondered if he would be disappointed in how it all turned out between my aunts, uncles and me.

Then, I started to remember what my Grandpa had said to me in private at least 10 years earlier when I was visiting with my birth mother one day. My aunts and uncles were in my older aunt's kitchen, they were eating, talking loudly and laughing as normal. My Grandpa said, "Can you hear your aunts and uncles talking?" and I nodded. I could hear them, but I couldn't understand what they were talking about because they were talking in their native language. Grandpa said, "They think because I'm bedridden that I can't hear them. It's my legs that don't work, not my ears. Your older aunt's husband is the smartest one of them all because he doesn't talk like them; their tongues are evil. They only know how to gossip. I love them but I continue to pray for my children." I also remembered my Grandpa telling me, "When I'm gone, they won't want you anymore. They are only nice to you because I tell them you are my favorite out of all our family because you were the grandchild your Grandmother and I brought up as our own, you were our little girl. You are my granddaughter, but I love you. I know my adult children, and they are only nice to you because they know how much I love you." I remembered telling my Grandpa not to worry about it because all my aunts and uncles loved me but at the time he patted my hand and said, "I know my children better than they know themselves."

Mind Reading

When I was nearly 22, I came up with a plan. I planned on buying a house. I had a new boyfriend, the relationship only lasted two years but at the time I thought that one day we would be married. He also wanted to buy a house, so we planned on buying a house and to move in together after we got married

I was working several jobs to help pay for my share of the house deposit. One of those jobs included waitressing at a local a-la-carte restaurant about 10 mins from my home that I lived in alone.

The shifts at the restaurant were always in the evening and because I was a night owl, I enjoyed these dinner shifts. I'd come into work about 5:30pm before all the dinner guests started arriving at 6:00pm. The job included me setting up all the tables with fresh linen, folding napkins into a shell design, making sure the cutlery for all the tables were polished, taking food orders and delivering them to the tables.

One night, as I was folding napkins to put on the table, the owner of the restaurant came to see me. He pointed to a man with a turban on his head and said this man wanted to speak to me. I said that I don't know him. I was busy folding napkins before the dinner service was due to start. The owner told me this man was here to tell me my fortune. He could tell me my future. He explained how this man had shown up to his restaurant unannounced two years before and told him to move his restaurant to the other side of the road to be successful and because of this fortune teller's advice, the owner had moved his restaurant across the street and become a millionaire. I still said, "No," but the owner was adamant and told me I would still get paid when I went to see this fortune teller. The owner explained, this was the first time this fortune teller had come back in two years. So, I put down the napkins I was folding and went to see him.

We met in a separate room away from the main dining room. The fortune teller sat on the opposite side of the table to me and told me he could read my mind and tell me my future. I was sceptical but because the owner of the restaurant was paying for me to sit with him, I listened to what this fortune teller was saying. He gave me three small pieces of paper; they were each the same size as one half of a raffle ticket. He also gave me a pen.

He asked me to write down a color, any color, and he would tell me what the color was. I thought of crimson; it wasn't an ordinary color that he could guess. Then he said, "Your colour is crimson." I was annoyed at how he knew the correct answer. Then he said to write down any number from 1 to 100. I covered my hand as I wrote the answer so small on the check ticket in case he was trying to cheat but he guessed correctly. Then he asked me to write down any flower, and I thought of a flower. I wrote it down, covering my hand without looking at what I wrote, staring at him to see how he was cheating but again he guessed correctly.

He told me about my birth mother; he told me her full name. It wasn't a common name; it was an islander name and consisted of at least 10 letters, yet he knew her name and pronounced it correctly. He started to tell me about my childhood, things no stranger would ever know. He told me I was looking to buy a house with a boyfriend, and I said that's not true, but he became angry and correctly stated the house number and street name and told me to stop trying to lie to him because he could read my mind. He proceeded to tell me when I was getting married; how miserable my life was going to be in that marriage and the age I would die and how I would die. He told me that he knew all these things because he could read my mind and tell me about my future.

He sat smiling to himself after 30 minutes of telling me about how miserable my life ahead of me was going to be and asked me to compensate him for his time. In my mind I said, "Is $5, ok? If you can read my mind is $5 alright?" But he said nothing, so I pulled out $5 from my pocket, put it on the table and left the room while he became enraged at me for only putting $5 on the table. He couldn't read my mind at all, otherwise he would have said something when in my mind as I looked at him, I was saying is $5 ok, yet he never replied. Serves him right for trying to scam me, I thought to myself.

My boyfriend and I broke up not long after we bought the house together. He moved into the house with a male friend and said he was renovating it before he planned to propose and for us to get married, but he did no renovations in months. The thoughts of that fortune teller came to mind. I started watching this boyfriend openly flirt with other women while we dated and lie to me, so I ended the relationship and transferred the house to him for $1 on the proviso that we never had any further contact.

Some years later after I met my wonderful husband and we had children the thought of that fortune teller came to mind every now and again. I counted down the days to my death because he told me the age that I would die. It often scared me. I never told my husband about it at the time, but I wondered if people could actually tell me my future. It would be better for me if I knew ahead of time whether something was about to happen, that way I could be prepared and continue being in control.

If a clairvoyant, psychic or medium was in town for a big show, I'd book tickets to go with a friend. It didn't matter the cost, but I wondered if one day they would choose me to tell my future, but they never did. I started searching for a clairvoyant, psychic or medium for a personal reading and found several in my area. I sought them out most years or when I was worried about something. They told me about things coming up for my work, new people I would meet and most of the time I wasn't allowed to record the conversations, but they offered pen and paper for me to make notes whilst they spoke. If they couldn't tell me anything then they would bring out tarot cards or I'd take off my wedding ring for them to hold for a more in-depth reading. I always left those appointments in tears because they'd give me updates about my dead relatives, yet I couldn't stop myself from seeing them.

It gave me comfort to know what was happening in my life, and what my dead relatives thought about my life. I was grateful to know the age I was going to die because then I could plan for it. However, every time I thought about it, I would always become sad thinking how my husband and children would feel about me dying and attending my funeral. I hoped that one day, if God really existed, that He would see I was a good person and allow me into heaven because that's where my Grandparents would be.

Getting Married

My future husband and I met through mutual friends. I'd moved to live with two girlfriends. The three of us young woman lived together but my two flatmates worked together for the same company. I'd known one of them since I was 14. We all got on like sisters; it was wonderful and I loved living with them.

It was the backyard party that I had no interest in going to but one of my flatmates told me about a guy she knew and wanted me to meet. She said he was perfect for me, but I trusted in myself and reminded my friend I went to VIP parties and night clubbing not a backyard party. All my night clubbing friends were sick. I wondered how they were all sick at the same time. Phone call after phone call, they all sounded terrible and had the flu and couldn't go out. It had been about seven months since my Grandpa had passed away and I had cut ties with most of my family. I'd chosen to be single during that time but now I was single and ready to mingle.

I didn't want to finish work and just go home because it was the weekend. I knew about the backyard party that my friend had mentioned. It was at one of her co-worker's homes and she explained all the staff from her work were coming. I decided to go.

The taxi took me to the address that my friend gave me. The street was crowded with cars; the backyard was loud as I walked in and people from her work were everywhere. They were all chatting loudly, laughing, drinking, and a few people were dancing to the music. My friend was waiting for me as I walked in, and she gestured for me to come over. I walked in and sat next to her. I hadn't been there for five minutes when a tall, handsome guy walked over and asked if I wanted a beer. I nodded and said, "Yes, thank you," as though he was a waiter. He brought me back a beer and I looked at it wondering why he didn't bring me a glass. I abruptly told him I needed a glass and he went and got one. We chatted briefly and I finished the beer. He was very handsome, but I didn't want to give him the wrong idea because I was here to meet the person my friend told me that would be my perfect match.

As he walked away, my friend said, "What do you think?" The guy I'd just spent time talking to was the person she wanted to introduce me to. He was talking to someone else now and I decided that I'd blown it. He was incredibly handsome and I wondered why my friend didn't tell me sooner that this was the person she wanted me to meet. I pulled out some VIP tickets for a new nightclub opening, I'd been invited to and suggested to my friend that since the guy she wanted me to meet was now talking to another girl that maybe we could leave. We left and I waved goodbye to the tall handsome guy thinking that I wouldn't see him again because I seemed uninterested in him when we spoke.

A few weeks passed and my other flatmate said she had been approached by a guy at her work who was a friend. He told her that he'd met me at a backyard party and wanted to know if he could have my number. I nodded calmly and said he could. It was that tall handsome guy I'd met at the backyard party; my heart was pounding so fast. I thought he didn't like me.

We dated for about seven months. We decided from the start it couldn't be a relationship of lust, as we both wanted to get to know each other and this included no holding hands and no kissing for at least three months. During that time, I realized this was the first time I'd ever felt so much love for a boyfriend. It was the first time I imagined a happy and fulfilling life with anyone. He felt the same so we decided to go overseas on a holiday, just the two of us to see if we could actually still get along by seeing each other every day. We enjoyed a week in Hawaii together. I didn't want to be away from him after that. We came back to our separate homes, and I started thinking about us getting married.

I went to multiple jewellery stores and found engagement rings I liked at each shop. I got each of the stores to write the name, design, cost and my ring finger size on a business card. I gave all of them to my boyfriend and said when he was ready to propose to me that these were the rings I'd picked out that he could choose from. He looked surprised but laughed. He told me that if he was going to do that, it would be confidential.

About a year after we started dating, he proposed with one of the rings I'd given him details of from the jewellery store business cards. I instantly said, "Yes," because I'd found my prince charming. I wanted a family of our own, I wanted to celebrate with friends, but I didn't know what to do about my family.

Only a very small number of my family were invited to our wedding. I was still too hurt to invite all of them. Then, as I tried on wedding dresses, I wondered how I would walk down the aisle because I had no father or family member to give me away at my wedding. I contemplated walking myself down the aisle. I was so happy to be marrying my prince charming, but I was so sad that I didn't have a family member who could walk me down the aisle. I spent a few nights alone in my room crying about it. I felt useless because the four uncles I had, I loved each of them like older brothers, but we were having a one-way Mexican standoff. I didn't invite them to my wedding because I was still angry with them because they didn't stick up for me regarding my Grandpa's funeral. They didn't call me about my wedding because I didn't tell any of them, I was getting married.

A week before the wedding, one of my uncles rang. He was the managing director of a satellite company, always travelling around the world for business meetings. He said he'd just found out that I was getting married and asked who would be walking me down the aisle. I told him no one, I was going to walk myself down the aisle at church. He said, "No, that's not right. I will change all my plans for you because I love you, I will fly in for your wedding, give you away as the representative for the family at church." At the reception he said he could only stay a short time before he had to fly back overseas that day for another meeting. I cried tears of joy.

On the day of our wedding, my uncle walked me down the aisle, gave an emotional and heartfelt speech at our wedding and was then met by government officials to take him to the airport as a VIP so he could board his flight to attend his next meeting overseas.

My husband and I had a wonderful wedding with 100 of our closest family and friends. Nearly 30 years have passed since then. To date I'm still the luckiest person to have met this amazing man.

Maybe that prayer as an 8-year-old on the bathroom floor, crying silently that if I ever survived that house of torture, if I ever lived to be an adult that I would one day hopefully have a family who loved me. I wondered after my wedding if it was all a coincidence about meeting this perfect man for me as my soul mate or whether God had heard my prayer from when I was eight years old.

My Heart Smiled

My husband and I found out we were having a baby. We didn't search for a girl's name. We only did searches for a boy's name. When my Grandma died when I was eight years old, I always planned that if I was lucky enough to have a daughter, I would name her after my Grandma.

I was having morning sickness from three weeks of being pregnant. The nausea was under control from eating food, but the vomiting was so strong, I thought I'd throw the baby up. I went to see my doctor, as I was very concerned about how sick I was and he told me my baby was taking control of the nourishment it needed and not to worry. He also confirmed there was no way I could vomit a baby out of my mouth while I was pregnant and not to worry about the morning sickness because it would stop by 12 weeks.

I went back to visit my doctor regularly about my pregnancy. I saw the doctor at 12 weeks and when the morning sickness hadn't stopped he told me again not to worry. The baby was fine and sometimes the morning sickness could last past 12 weeks. I was irritated by this doctor. Why didn't he just say he didn't know how long the morning sickness would last? He assured me my baby was fine and told me to make sure, due to my severe morning sickness, that I had plenty of rest.

When the doctor told me to rest he meant to take it easy, but I interpreted it as not to exhaust myself in any capacity. I thought it was ok to spend days that turned into weeks and months of just eating and no exercise. One day I went for a walk with a friend - I was only five months pregnant at this stage. As we walked slowly, I felt my legs were so itchy. I had to keep stopping to scratch them by putting my hands down the length of my pants but the itching did not stop. I made another appointment for the doctor and told him what had happened when I went for a short walk with a friend. He asked me what exercise I'd done in the last few months, and I proudly told him how I'd not done anything; I'd rested like he told me. I expected the doctor to say that's wonderful but instead he said, "When I told you to rest, I didn't mean to do nothing but eat and lay down for months." I asked the doctor if I had harmed my baby because the itching on my legs was severe from the short walk I did with a friend. The doctor said the reason for the itching was due to circulation because I'd been too lazy for so long.

I watched a lot of romantic comedy movies during my pregnancy, of people finding their true love, getting married and having a baby and a family of their own. One of the best parts of those movies was how the woman left hospital skinnier than when she was pregnant. Their stomachs just sucked back to normal. I made a mental note to myself that when my baby was due to be born, I'd pack a pair of my old skinny pants I wore before I was ever pregnant. This baby was going to be huge I thought as I'd already put on 20 kilos, I felt so clever.

The time was fast approaching for our baby to be born. My husband and I went to our ultrasound appointment at 20 weeks, and we told them we didn't want to know the sex of our baby. We wanted it as a surprise but I knew it would be a boy because this baby kicked with such strength, it could only be a boy to be that strong.

Labor pains started early one day while I was out walking with some friends. I rang my husband and he took me to the hospital. The midwife announced, "Congratulations your baby is healthy." I asked if I could see my son and she said, "You've had a daughter."

I looked at my little baby girl's face, so beautiful, so precious. I couldn't believe how perfect she was. This tiny human was mine; I was responsible for her. It was like my heart had smiled for the first time.

As my baby girl grew, she showed her father and me about the joy of having children. Our daughter loved to love others. She was very affectionate and always told us how much she loved us. She was very determined and she was confident in everything she did. I thought about how motherhood had calmed me and I wanted to protect my daughter from everything that could hurt her. If someone looked at my daughter the wrong way I confronted them about it. If anyone spoke disrespectfully about my daughter, I cut them out of our lives so they could never be disrespectful again.

When our daughter was four she attended day care. The teachers at her day care told me she was ready for big kid's school. Children didn't start school until they were five but they told me she was ready. I was so proud of our baby girl for being so clever. I found the closest Catholic primary school to our home to enrol her. My husband asked why a Catholic school as neither of us were Catholics, and we didn't go to church, but I told him it was because I wanted our daughter to know about God. I couldn't explain God to my daughter because I didn't know if God was real, but I trusted the Catholic school and thought how they could explain it to her. She was smart and would understand what I couldn't understand at her age.

There are so many wonderful memories of being a Mum for the first time because of my precious daughter. I went to great lengths to make sure her world was perfect. Every toy she ever wanted, I bought it. Everything her heart desired, I wanted that for her too. Every year she had a birthday party because I never wanted her to feel like how I felt at 13 years of age. For her 12th birthday I painted her bedroom, I had new floors installed at our home and confirmed it was no problem if she wanted 12 of her school friends to come to our home for a modelling party and sleepover. She wanted a day of pretending they were models. I had a friend who was a professional makeup artist come to the party to do all their makeup, another friend who loved photography came and took photos then gifted their photos to them as a memento of their time together at my daughter's 12th birthday. I wasn't going overboard with birthday parties; I was just too triggered from my past to ever let it affect my daughter.

As the years progressed, the parties became larger too. My daughter explained at 17 that she wanted to invite her closest friends to our home. No problem, I thought. When 90 of her closest friends turned up, I just organized at least 20 boxes of takeaway pizzas to be delivered to our home for all of them to eat. Later that night, when my cigarettes went missing from our back deck (from the hiding spot that I hid them in the corner) I realized one of her friends had stolen my packet of cigarettes and I was furious about it. "How dare they, I thought to myself." I announced to her 90 closest friends that if they didn't bring my missing cigarette packet back, the party was being shut down in 10 minutes. I didn't notice I did anything wrong when I shut the party down later by screaming at others because I was protecting my own home from a thief.

My daughter finished high school and worked at a job she chose. She went out with friends she wanted in her life. She was capable, she was beautiful, but she was still my baby girl. Every time she smiled, I loved her and was happy that she was happy. Every time she laughed it was so contagious that I couldn't help but laugh too even if I didn't know what she was laughing about. Every time she was sad, I wanted to drive to that person's home who had made her upset and scream at them until they apologized.

I looked at my daughter and saw a young woman who was strong. Those kicks she did while I was pregnant with her showed her strength. She was physically strong, mentally capable and ready to step into the world as a young woman.

As I watched our daughter grow, she continued to amaze me. She was quick witted like her Dad and she was funny like her brother. She loved others easily and I was thankful that she was nothing like me. She didn't get angry easily, she didn't find faults with others, she didn't make excuses when things went wrong, and she always walked with love and kindness.

One day I sat and thought how lucky I am to have her as my daughter. To this day, I look at her and every time I still think how, because of my precious baby girl, my heart smiled.

Angie From Accounts

I worked for a telecommunications company. When I started, I was about the 50th staff member. I didn't go to a job interview for the role but instead my manager had been head hunted and he asked me to come across with him, and it included more money! I would no longer work in a call centre taking abusive calls from customers who had restrictions placed on their mobile phones due to unpaid bills, so I agreed. My manager was a talker; he loved talking about himself. He was a little crude but at least he got the job done. We'd worked together for a few years at the call center, and he was always approachable if any customers were overly abusive over the phone. I wasn't the only person who transferred with him. It was nice to have my team leader from the call centre also transfer across to this new business.

I was working for less than three months in accounts when I was told we would be going on strike. I asked other staff members in my department and was told the strike was because the other ladies in my department didn't like our manager. They labelled him sleazy and crude while I labelled him as just a boss who told silly jokes and talked about himself. I didn't hold any offence to him but the rest of our team did. I was told that we would not be coming into work. The accounts team would be on strike if the company we all worked for continued to employ our current manager. I disagreed, I was coming into work to get paid, I got this new job because of my manager, and I'm not going on any strike.

Within the next few days my manager was no longer my boss; the company had let him go due to pressure by other staff members. My old team leader was now our team leader. I watched my old team leader talk lovingly and caring to all the old staff in our department; there was something off with her. Had she intentionally caused everyone to be offended by our old boss? I wondered, so I kept my guard up around her.

I worked doing what I was told in those days. We weren't a close-knit team, but all the work got done. I started to review different processes we were doing in accounts and passed suggestions to my team leader. She shrugged them off as though they were all terrible ideas.

After a year of working for my team leader, I went on unpaid maternity leave a month before my due date but came back to work when our son was four months old as we needed the money. My son was sick from two months of age. The stress made me turn back to cigarettes. He was bottle fed now so both my husband and I could feed him. The daycare he went to was the same place his sister went to; they were excellent with both my kids. As I calmed down so did our son.

On my return to work, I found the telecommunications company had grown to 250 staff. We'd relocated to a new building over two floors. The ground floor was a call center and the second floor was where all admin staff, managers, our CFO and CEO worked. I was upstairs working in accounts.

From the moment I returned to work I focused on getting away from my team leader, who had been promoted to manager during my short maternity leave. I didn't want to be let go by the company because she didn't like me. I wanted to be away from her, preferably managing my own team. I'd decided that instead of running ideas past my manager, I'd direct them straight to the CEO. I was quietly sick of my manager taking credit for things I'd done and being rude to me at other times. I held a grudge against her because I also felt she was holding me back.

I was promoted within a short period of time from all my ideas to the CEO and now I managed three separate departments. I made certain that each of my departments worked efficiently. My rudeness towards anyone who disrespected me in the workplace or my teams was well known by all staff on the second floor and I was given the nickname at work of: "Angie, the dragon lady from accounts." I remember the first time I was told by a staff member in my team about my nickname. I laughed because others were intimidated by me but really I was just trying to make sure I had a job that was able to pay the bills. I feared being fired. The more departments I managed, the more money I earnt. It didn't matter what others said to me at work, it only mattered what my little family thought. It didn't matter what others thought about me being ruthless, I was prepared to fight with anyone and everyone if KPIs were not met or things were done wrong. I was answerable now to the General Manager, CFO and CEO, not my old team leader.

I went downstairs one day to have a smoke break. I stood just staring at the sky and having a cigarette when a young woman walked towards me in the smoking area. I smiled and said, "Hello." I told her I hadn't seen her before and she said she worked in the call center on the ground floor. We talked for a while as we both smoked our cigarettes and she asked where I worked. I told her I worked upstairs on the second level. She said eagerly, "Do you know about the dragon lady on that level?" I knew she was talking about me but decided to play along. I shook my head to say no and replied, "Who is that?" She proceeded to tell me a whole range of stories of things the dragon lady in accounts had done. As she told stories I just listened but, in my mind, I was thinking yes that part is true, wow that part is totally fabricated. The legend of Angie from accounts had become quite extravagant at my workplace and I didn't want to let down the persona, so I could continue to get the job done because most people feared Angie, the dragon lady from accounts, I was very results driven.

The young woman said, "Do you know that girl Angie from accounts?" I nodded as I took a long drawn-out puff of my cigarette. Out of 250 staff, I was the only person in the whole company with the name Angie who worked in accounts. The young woman told me how lovely it was to meet me; she'd enjoyed our chat and maybe we could catch up again. I nodded as she spoke. She reminded me to be careful of Angie in accounts and I nodded again! She said, "What's your name?"

I said, "Angie," and a look of worry came across her entire face. "What department do you work in?" she asked as I took a big puff of my cigarette.

Then I said, "Accounts," and her eyes widened. She realized in that moment she was talking to Angie the dragon lady from accounts. She turned and ran; she ran back into the building while I chuckled to myself. I told my friends at work, and we all laughed about the look on that young girl's face. I never saw her again after that.

Panic In The Back Seat

My son was now in high school. He had a girl he liked but I disliked her from the moment I met her because she'd taught my son how to lie to me.

Everyone knew the one thing I couldn't handle was lies. Specifically, because my birth mother was a liar, so I distanced myself from anyone like her. People at work knew it, family and friends knew it too. If you disliked me, I was ok for you to tell me to my face and I'd make sure to keep my distance from you but if you were nice to my face then talked terrible about me behind my back, don't be surprised if I confronted you about it. This was my no-nonsense approach; it was called being as subtle as a head butt. It was the same for family and friends; there was no grey area. It was either the truth or a lie. If I didn't like you, I told you to your face. If I liked you then I made every effort to protect you and love you. If I loved you but you lied to me, you were out. I cut many people from my life because of lies or their disrespect towards any of my family or me. There were no three strikes and you're out policy; it was instant – you're out!

My son's girlfriend was a definite no for me. I told her to her face within minutes of meeting her. I didn't like her, but my son was older now and he was having none of my concern for him. He continued to date her; I wasn't happy about it, but I liked the fact he was honest with me about it. He didn't try to hide it, he just said, "I like her, and I've asked her to be my girlfriend. I've been honest with you about it, and I would like for you to get to know her." So I agreed. A few weeks later, my son's girlfriend came to our home for her first visit. My son appeared at the front door as though he knew the moment she was in our street. As she walked across our front lawn, he opened the door and said, "Hello," to her. She didn't look at me and then cowardly walked away with my son as he led her to his bedroom. Maybe she was intimidated by me, so I let it go. I thought that maybe I'd let her calm down a bit. My son's bedroom door was open; they'd have to come out at some stage to get food or a drink. After half an hour, nothing. I called out to them, but my son confirmed they were fine. These visits continued for weeks.

My son's girlfriend would now come in the front door, run to my son's room without acknowledging any of us who lived there. That was just rude, I thought, but said nothing. I could always hear them talking so I knew nothing was going on. I wondered if my son's girlfriend was so scared of me and that's why they spent all their time in his small bedroom together. I walked into his bedroom and as soon as my son's girlfriend saw me, she stopped talking. I said, "Hello," but she didn't respond. "Ok, let it go," I thought to myself. "She's just shy so best to leave it until she became more familiar."

After six months of my son and his girlfriend dating, I asked my daughter what she thought about her brother's girlfriend. My daughter said she didn't have an opinion because her brother's girlfriend had never spoken to her. They'd sat in the loungeroom together before, but my son's girlfriend would never talk to her. So, in six months I thought, my daughter who is an amazing human, so caring, gentle, happy, full of love was also tagged as unapproachable by my son's girlfriend. That was rubbish, this has to be an act. I could understand anyone not liking me but to not even talk to me or be respectful to my daughter in my daughter's own home, that was definitely not on.

Through my son, I found out his girlfriend was a vegetarian, so I made an effort to find dishes that I thought she'd like, but she didn't like any of them. I researched recipes and cooked them for her when she visited but she still wouldn't eat any of them. I found out from my son that the only meal she liked was hot chips. It didn't matter if the hot chips had chicken salt on it or not, but hot chips were the only meal she ate when she came over. If I knew she was coming over, I'd pre-order hot chips for her before she arrived from our local fish and chip shop as they were her favorite. She also liked the hot chips from McDonald's. We had hot chips with lots of meals whenever my son's girlfriend came over.

My son's girlfriend was now causing my own children to fight. My son couldn't understand why his big sister made no effort to get to know his girlfriend, but my son couldn't understand that his girlfriend was deliberately causing the rift. He just couldn't understand why they didn't get on. I thought it was ridiculous, as I watched on in silence. That afternoon my son asked me to drive his girlfriend home. My son and his girlfriend hopped into the back seat. Even though the back seat accommodated three persons, they sat in the middle and side seat so they could hold hands while I drove her home. I looked in the rear vision mirror and saw her looking at me. She quickly looked away. I decided to start a conversation with her, if she wasn't going to say anything to me. It had now been more than six months of nothing but a hello or goodbye from each of us. She'd said less to my daughter, and it made me cranky that she was so rude to my beautiful daughter.

At the first red light on the 20-minute drive back to her home. I turned to look in the back seat and as my son's girlfriend looked at me, I said, "Did my son ever tell you I come from a big family?" She shook her head, still not using her words. I said, "Our last family reunion, we had 300 people turn up." She just looked at me blankly but said nothing so I continued. "That 300 is only from my Grandpa's side of the family, then we have my immediate family of aunts, uncles and cousins with their families, that would be another 100 people," I said, and she still didn't say anything. I told her how my family was so diverse. We came in shades of albino to 10 minutes to midnight. We came in all sizes too from four foot tall to more than six foot tall. We came in shapes of small framed to the size of a fridge and we lived all over the world," but my son's girlfriend still said nothing.

My son said, "Mum, why are you saying this?"

I answered with a smile as I continued to drive his girlfriend home, "Because I want your girlfriend to know that anyone I love, I love deeply and will protect them." I now looked at his girlfriend, our eyes met in the rear vision mirror and I said, "Let me remind you, while you go out with my son and he's happy then we don't have a problem but if you intend to hurt him or anyone else he loves then know this, I will come after you. I will intentionally hunt you down. I'll do it through family and because my family is so large you won't know when or where. Do I make myself clear?"

She looked at me then put her hands up to her face. My son said, "Mum, she's having a panic attack. Just stop!" That's odd, why would I stop? I was just getting started.

Not long after, my son and his girlfriend broke up. I was blamed for the break-up, but I was more than happy about it. My children went back to talking to each other again. I thought it was wonderful that I could prevent my own children severing ties with each other. I gave myself a pat on the back for my efforts.

My Time Is Relevant

My husband and I owned a collectible vehicle. It was my husband's pride and joy. I tell you, if that car had boobs, he would have spent more time with it than me. He loved his car. He spent time polishing it and he enjoyed driving in it and enjoyed talking about it. Secretly, I didn't like the car. It was over 20 years old and falling apart. How does a married man with two children own a two-door vehicle? I'd tell others, it's because he has an awesome wife!

We took my husband's car everywhere. The kids loved it because the back seats matched the front seats; it had bucket seats like a racing car to sit in but the car was quietly falling apart. The interior leather on the doors was coming off and the material on the ceiling was dropping down but the engine was great and had no mechanical problems. My car was the opposite; it had been having a lot of mechanical issues, but the inside wasn't falling apart, and it was a seven-seater not a four-seater. Second or third hand vehicles was what we did, buying them through a bank loan or dealership car finance because we couldn't afford a new car.

One day, my husband noticed a new car he really liked. It was a utility vehicle but could seat five. It was much higher off the ground than his 4-seater, and it had embroidery on the front seats. It was a chunky looking car but I had to admit this utility vehicle was a good-looking car. We went to the car dealership to have a look. Window shopping for a new car was ok. I could tell my husband really wanted this new car. I liked that it was a normal five-seater vehicle instead of his four-seater; it had four doors instead of two doors. I was glad that he was finally ready to get rid of his old car. The salesperson came over and my husband chatted with him. They talked about something called horsepower, cylinders, fuel capacity. The salesperson opened the car door and we both looked inside. I walked away for a bit because the conversation about cars was too complicated for me to understand but I had to admit the stitching on the headrest of this new car was lovely; it was a nice car. I watched as my husband fell in love with this car. "Good," was my thought, "we can finally get rid of his four-seater." The salesperson asked, "Do you have a trade in vehicle?" My husband nodded as I smiled - goodbye four-seater old car.

"Yes, my husband replied, "I have a seven-seater car I'd like to trade in."

My smile vanished. "No, not my car," I said. "He has an old car."

Then I started telling the salesperson about my husband's old four-seater vehicle but he said, "You can't sell that, it's a collectible vehicle."

"Right," I thought. They'd obviously talked about this while I walked off as they spoke about cylinders and fuel capacity. "I'm not trading in my car," I told the two of them. I started walking away and my husband laughed.

I heard him tell the salesperson, "My wife won't part with her car, and I won't part with mine, so thanks anyway," and they shook hands. My husband thanked him for his time and we left. He was a bit cheeky, my husband, but he was so handsome, loving and kind. I didn't deserve him, but I loved him and he could do no wrong.

A few months went by, and my husband was still thinking about that five-seater car. He decided we should look to see if they had any second-hand options available, it would be cheaper for us, so we went to other car dealerships in our area to have a look. We found one about 20 minutes from our home. It was exactly what my husband wanted. Low kilometers, good mileage, excellent interior and only two years old. The price was a lot more affordable; we still had to get a loan to buy it. We walked into the dealership, and a young man came over. I stood quietly as my husband told him what he was looking for. The salesperson asked, "Do you have a trade-in vehicle?" My husband nodded and told him about his four-seater car. Yes!!!!, we are finally getting rid of that old four-seater - this was going to be a great day. The salesperson showed us to a room. He offered us water, tea and coffee but we only wanted to make enquiries and get an updated quote after trade in price was organised. We still had to work on our finances to see what we could afford. I was happy, my husband was happy. It was a happy day as we both sat and chatted as we waited for the salesperson who had left the room to return with the updated price after my husband's four-seater was to be traded in.

I sat patiently as the salesperson every 10 minutes, kept popping his head into the room to say, "Not much longer," and asked us if we wanted anything to drink. We both shook our heads and said, "No."

I looked at the clock hanging on the wall and realized my husband and I had been in this room for 20 minutes. I started to become impatient. I looked at my husband's face and could tell the sparkle of delight he had when we first walked in had started to fade. No one upsets my husband, I thought to myself, I'd stand up for him. The salesperson popped his head back into the room at that moment with the usual, "Not much longer," as he prepared to dart out again. "No!" I shouted to him as I tapped my husband's knee. "We have been sitting here for 20 minutes. I don't want excuses from you, I want results. You have 20 minutes to organize yourself with this updated quote or we are leaving." The salesperson nodded, apologized, and smiled. He told us how my husband's old car needed to be valued. They were on the phone with other car dealerships to check on a price they could sell it for before they could provide us with an updated sale price for the second hand five-seater. What a load of rubbish! As the salesperson finished speaking I said, "Your time starts now," and I set a timer on my phone for 20 minutes.

A salesperson continued to pop their head in but now it was every five minutes. "Not much longer," they said then asked if we wanted anything to drink. We both shook our heads. I turned the volume up on my phone. It won't be long now till my alarm goes off. How dare these people at this car dealership treat my husband with such disrespect, making him wait over 30 minutes in a room while they sorted themselves out. I looked at my husband; I could tell he'd now lost all interest in the car, but he didn't like confrontation. I patted his knee again and smiled as I thought, that I've got this; no one is upsetting my husband. The alarm on my mobile phone went off. I let it echo through the dealership so all the salespeople at this dealership knew to come into our room that we'd obediently sat in for 40 minutes. "Is everything ok?" asked the salesperson as we got up to leave. "Where are you going?" The salesperson asked as my husband and I went to leave. I looked at the salesperson, smiled and said, "Your 20 minutes are up!" We walked towards the exit and the salesperson came running to apologize for the time he took to get the quote together. As he pleaded with me, he tried to hand me a piece of paper with the updated quote - I looked at my husband.

"No thanks," my husband said. "I've lost interest now." and we both turned and walked out of the dealership. We held hands leaving that car dealership. My husband lost interest in that utility vehicle, and I was glad that I could show that car dealership that my time was relevant. To date, we still have that old four-seater car.

CHAPTER 3

COVETING WHAT WASN'T MINE

A SHORT SERIES OF RANDOM ANGRY ANGE STORIES

Pram Push Or $15,000

My husband and I married and we moved interstate. We had a beautiful baby girl, and I was a stay-at-home Mum. I didn't have any friends or family around when our daughter was nine months old, so I started attending a pram push group. All the young mums would turn up at a designated spot so we could all walk together while pushing our children in their prams. We'd stop at a park along the way so our young toddlers could all play together. Then we would end up at a coffee shop, order coffees and talk some more about how we were coping being mothers, and talk about our family life and our struggles. We did this twice a week. At the start I really enjoyed it but then some of the Mums would whinge about their partners. I had nothing to whinge about; my husband was amazing. He was a wonderful provider, a wonderful father and an amazing husband. Some talked about their partners successes. They sounded encouraging for a while until I felt like I was less than them as a parent for not being able to have all the nice things everyone else had. I started having thoughts that they were judging me, even though they probably weren't.

My husband and I were renting a small house, but we were happy. We made plans for the future that one day, even though we had nothing now, we might have our own home instead of renting. I started coming home early from pram push groups. They were all lovely, too lovely for me I suppose but I had nothing left to contribute to their conversations. So instead of staying for the walk, park and coffee I just started doing the walk, and park and then back home. My husband asked about my pram push groups and I told him I was coming home early. I didn't want drama in my own life but I was happy watching it, in particular Days of our Lives and Young and the Restless. He said it wasn't healthy so I tried to keep doing the pram push groups for a few more months but started watching recorded episodes of Days of our Lives and Young and the Restless while our daughter had her day sleep. Watching daytime soaps was exciting until my husband reminded me it wasn't healthy, so I stopped my binge-watching of daytime soap opera shows and thought about ways to make money while he was at work. I wanted what others had for my family; at the very least I wanted us to have our own home instead of renting.

Our daughter loved dancing, so I started putting the radio on after she woke up from her day sleep. For the first time I heard about a radio competition called Secret Sound. They repeated the sound every day and each day they gave a new clue. Callers would phone in and give answers to what they thought the secret sound was but if no one guessed the sound the prize money increased, it was already at $10,000. I started keeping notes and trying to distinguish what the secret sound could be. I stopped going to pram push groups so I wouldn't miss a single clue.

One weekend my husband and I went to look at a new housing development near our home. The homes were lovely, even though the land plots themselves were small, but it was a chance to have our own piece of real estate. We went to another new housing development but because the plots of land were bigger, the homes were also larger and the deposit was $20,000. It was a wonderful dream but realistically we couldn't afford it and I became envious of what others had and kept thinking about what we were missing out on.

We'd started to try and save money, but it wasn't nearly enough. I thought about the Secret Sound radio competition and decided I would try harder during the week. During the week I went through all the clues again. I felt like Sherlock Holmes after the victory of solving a case. I had the Secret Sound radio competition down to two possibilities and waited for the next time the radio station said for callers to call through to have a guess. Everyone would always ring at that moment, and you were lucky to hear the line ring when you called, but most times it was a busy tone, and I was unable to get through due to the large volume of calls. I organized my daughter with all her toys, so she was happy while I waited to call the radio station.

As soon as the radio station said to call now, I picked up my landline and pressed redial. I'd called them already earlier that morning and just hung up so the radio station number could be stored on my landline phone. That way when they said to call now, I didn't have to press each of the numbers to dial the radio station, I only had to press one button – redial. I was proud of myself for planning ahead. The line rang and the radio host said, "Hello, who do we have on the line?" I told them my name. Then they said, "Angie for $15,000 can you tell us what the secret sound is?"

I said, "It's one of two possibilities. Can I have two guesses for getting through first?"

But the radio host laughed and said, "No, sorry only one guess per call."

I took a deep breath and said, "Is it brushing your hair?"

The radio host said, "Can you please clarify, brushing your hair with what?"

I said, "Brushing your hair with a brush."

The radio host said, "No, sorry your answer is wrong." I hung up the phone so I could quickly redial and tell them my second possibility for the secret sound - it had to be brushing your hair with a comb.

As I pressed redial on the landline again, I heard the radio show continue. The second caller was through, and the radio host asked the same question to the second caller, "Hello, who do we have on the line?"

The man said, "It's Mark."

Then the radio host said, "Mark for $15,000 can you tell us what the secret sound is?"

Mark replied, "I like the answer for the first caller so is it brushing your hair with a comb?" I sat frozen staring at the radio.

The radio host said, "Mark, congratulations you've won $15,000" I started to cry and, in my mind, I was screaming, "Why?" I had failed my husband and our daughter because I said brush instead of comb. I'd lost out on $15,000. We had no way of paying for any deposit on our own home now.

I went to the bathroom and threw away both the brush and comb from the drawer in frustration then I had to retrieve them from the bin later so I could brush my daughter's hair that night and comb out the knots on my own head. I stopped listening to the radio for a while after that and only listened to CDs for music my daughter liked because listening to the radio made me feel like a loser. I wondered why good things, like winning money for a deposit for a home only happen for other people and not me.

Major Prize On My Radar

Our first cruise was coming up. My family and I had never been on a cruise ship before, and I was excited to be taking our little family of four away on holidays. A week visiting different islands in the pacific across seven days.

All food, drinks and accommodation were included for the bargain price of $1,000 as a total for my husband, myself and our two teenage children. Our friends were coming with us; they also had two children. All eight of us were excited about our holiday together.

Checking to board was easy, now all we had to do was find our cabin. We had an ocean view room with two sets of bunk beds. The kids both opted for the top bunks and my husband and I were quietly relieved because neither of us wanted to be climbing metal railings to get to bed each night

Day one on the ship was exciting. My friend and my husband pretended like they had randomly bumped into each other and people were smiling thinking what a lovely surprise for friends not knowing they were on the same holiday. Others didn't know we drove up in two cars following each other but after more drinks and random bumping into each other and looking surprised and other scenarios, everyone who was watching had caught on and looked away. That night, the eight of us went to dinner in the main dining room together. It was lovely and the meals were delicious. After an exhausting first day, we all went to bed.

The following morning, I was looking for a decent cup of coffee, not the one that was offered in the buffet area. I needed a proper caffeine hit to wake up properly after a bumpy first night. I ordered my coffee and felt lucky to find a vacant table of four, so I sat down. Not long after, a couple asked if they could sit at my table as they were also waiting for coffee. We began to chat and they told me how wonderful their lives were. How they'd been on at least 20 cruises with this cruise line, and dozens more cruises with other cruise lines. It seemed that regardless of what I brought up, they had done it, they were better at it, they'd achieved more and they knew everything. The lady said, "I'll let you in on a little secret. There is a casino on this ship and the major prizes for the poker machines need to be won before we all get back home." I thanked her for her tip. How lucky I thought that I'd bumped into them on day two instead of day seven. Now, I would have the funds to be able to go on more cruises like they did.

That afternoon, when everyone was lazing under the hot sun, I told my husband I was going for a walk. It was better to have some mystery on where I was going so I could later surprise him before we got off the ship with one of the major prizes from the poker machines in the casino.

The poker machine area was loud, some people were cheering while others were talking loudly at poker tables around the room. I surveyed the room and saw a poker machine with $20,000 as the major prize. "I'll win that one," I thought to myself, but it didn't accept cash. The casino cashier said all I had to do was tap my card and charge the amount I wanted to play onto my room card. It would add it as a charge to my cabin account. If I had any wins then all I had to do was come back to her, she would give me the cash, and I could deposit the funds through the customer service desk directly onto my account. It sounded easy enough.

So, I tapped my card and selected $20. After less than five minutes my $20 was gone. I tapped my card again, maybe I needed to play more, to win more I thought, so I tapped my room card again but this time selected $50, another 10 minutes passed and now my $50 was gone. Ok, I thought, I'll do it again, but this time select $100. No, that didn't work either I thought as the $100 disappeared within a short period of time. I thought that I must be on the wrong poker machine as I walked away to try my luck on a different poker machine where the major prize had not been won yet. Maybe I needed to bet more, maybe bet less, I thought. I had no idea what I was doing. I looked at my watch and wondered how long I'd been gone from my family and friends. It had been over an hour, so I rushed back to them before dinner.

That night, after we all went to bed, I kept thinking about the possibility of someone else winning what could be my major prize from the poker machine so I pretended to sleep while everyone else was still trying to fall asleep, but I kept one eye open watching the family and one eye closed pretending to be asleep. As I heard snoring, I opened both eyes and noticed everyone was asleep, I knew it was ok to get up without waking everyone. I got dressed and snuck out to go back to the casino. After a few hours of no wins, I snuck back into bed pretending like I hadn't gone out at all that night.

A few days went past. I continued spending time with my family and friends by day then I'd sneak out to the casino at night when my family were tucked away in bed fast asleep. By the fourth morning, I went to the customer service desk. I had no idea how much money I'd charged to our room account over the last couple of nights. I brought my sneaky credit card. The one my husband had no idea about. If the amount I'd charged to our room cabin account was too much then I'd reduce the value owing by paying with this secret credit card of mine - I felt so clever about bringing this card. "The value can't be labelled 'too much'," I thought to myself, as the customer service representative scanned my room card to get the total. I was wrong, it was extreme, it was ridiculous. I was out of control. I wondered what I was thinking as I started working out how to outsmart my husband. Ok, he can't know about this. The total value I'd spent in the last few days at the casino, plus a few small store purchases for the kids, was $1,635.45 cents. I'd been saving this secret credit card for a rainy day but now it felt like I was in the middle of a tornado storm. I gave the card to the customer service representative and asked her to apply payment of $1,600 to our room account. I knew my husband would question the account if they said it was a zero-balance owing. I felt quite clever and was proud of how sneaky I was.

I arrived at the buffet section on the top floor of the cruise ship. My husband, our kids and our friends were all waiting for me so we could have breakfast together. My husband asked where I'd been and I told him I went to check on our room account total. "That's funny," he said, "so did I." My eyes widened.

"How much was it?" I asked calmly as thoughts swirled around my brain so quickly. If he said $1,635.45 cents then he got the balance before I was able to pay it off with my secret credit card and I was in trouble BUT if he said $35.45, I was good. I was home free and had been so clever being sneaky that he'd never know. I'd pay that secret credit card off without him even knowing anything about it.

I looked casually at my husband full of confidence in myself as he replied, "They told me, it was $35.45." I smiled, I was so relieved, but my husband hadn't finished. He said, "I told customer service that if my wife was on a cruise ship for four days and had only spent $35.45, something was wrong. I asked them to print out every transaction." My smile stopped. He held up at least 8 x A4 sheets of paper and the only transactions you could see were casino, casino, casino. "You've been caught," I screamed at myself in my own mind as my eyes widened again.

He made me confess so I told him the truth; I told him how I'd met a couple in the cafe area. They'd told me about the major prizes and how I was sneaking out each night, including odd times during the day, when everyone else was busy. "What do you intend to do next?" he asked.

I confidently told him, "I was going to win it all back." They had poker tables and I was good at poker. He shook his head, but he made me promise not to go back into the casino without him. I agreed. That night, the kids went to kid's club. After kid's club, they went back to our cabin and watched a movie on the cabin TV while their parents went to the casino to win back all the money. We arrived and my husband gave me $100 cash.

He told me, "That is it. No more after that." I started telling the people at my poker table about my predicament. They all laughed. I started winning and soon I'd won $1,200. Each time I won anything I put the cashable poker chips in front of me and a hand would appear to my side and swipe them off the table; it was my husband keeping an eye on me. He was like my own special bodyguard. In total that night we won $1,700. I got up from the poker table, said, "Thank you," and reminded everyone that if I spent anymore time at this table or in the casino, I was going to be in trouble from my bodyguard. They all laughed!

Where was that know it all who knew about major prizes on a cruise ship? I wondered to myself, at how foolish I was to believe her. If I saw her again, I planned on either telling her what I thought of her or slapping her because of her lies. I felt like I'd been tricked but I couldn't see that I'd done anything wrong myself.

CHAPTER 4

LOSING CONTROL

A SHORT SERIES OF RANDOM ANGRY ANGE STORIES

Praying But Not Worthy

In life we meet people who we aren't related to by blood, but they become the family we choose for ourselves. I've been very lucky to have such people in my life. He started as a neighbor, and he had a beautiful wife and they had two beautiful daughters. Our birthdays were a day apart and I would joke and call him my brother from another mother and father. He and my husband were close friends and they chatted often. He had a big heart, and everyone loved him.

My friend's wife was like a ray of sunshine. I loved how she willingly loved others, and how, without trying, was the funniest person in the room, and she was the life of the party. She and her husband were high school sweethearts, and their daughters meant everything to them. They weren't lavish, they were just down to earth, happy, giving and loving friends. She was always there for me whenever I wanted to talk, and I made every effort to be there for her too.

One morning, as we went for our walk together, I noticed my friend looked worried so I asked her about it. She said her husband had been told he needed a heart transplant. He hadn't been in good health for some years but now his name had been registered as requiring a heart transplant. We talked as we walked; I was in disbelief that her husband who had the biggest heart I'd known, would require a new heart. I needed to be here for her. She was already strong, but she also had to be strong for her husband and daughters.

One night, she called excitedly to share that they had found a heart donor. Her husband had just been discharged from hospital, but he was about to go back in as a new heart had been found. I didn't know what to do so I remembered all the things I'd learnt from being a Catholic for so long. I started to pray for my friends.

"Dear God, can you please look after my friend. Can you please help him to be okay after surgery. Can you please help his wife to have enough strength for her family. Please help him to have a successful heart transplant so he is well again."

I prayed this same prayer every night, hoping if I was sincere in prayer that the God my Catholic school teachings had talked about would help my friend. I hoped my prayer would be answered. Several days passed and my friend's husband called my husband. He'd made it through surgery. He was calling to say Happy New Year; he was excited about the future because of his new heart. He said, "What doesn't kill you, makes you stronger." My husband and I were both overjoyed for him and his family.

A week later, while my husband and I were watching TV together one night and both our teenage children were in their bedrooms, there was loud knocking on our door. Who could it be? I thought it was so late, as I went to open the door. It was my beautiful friend. She didn't look happy, her smile was gone. Her eyes were swollen and she was shaking. We gestured for her to come in and sit down. She calmly explained that her husband's new heart didn't work anymore, and he had died earlier that day. We sat looking shocked. Didn't our friend only phone my husband from hospital during the week.? How did this happen? Another week went past and we went to our friend's funeral. More than 500 people turned up. He was very loved. We went to the funeral and then the wake, but I didn't know what to think. I was sad our friend died. How does someone with such a big heart die because of a heart problem? I was sad for his beautiful wife and their young daughters. Why? I kept saying to myself over and over. Why did this happen? He was such a good person, he was such a good friend. He had the biggest heart I'd ever known, yet it was his heart that failed.

The next day I realized why my friend died. It was because my prayers weren't good enough for the God other people talked about.

I'd always had this religious God as someone I prayed to every now and then when I needed something. I could understand why some things I prayed for, like winning the lottery, weren't answered but my friend's death was too much.

I stopped everything that I remembered being taught from my Catholic school days. It's all rubbish, I thought. Obviously, God was judging me for not being a good person. God didn't love me at all. This God that everyone else talked about just wasn't into me; I knew I had to clean myself up before saying any more prayers but emotionally, I'd lost control. It was too much. Best to stop praying when God doesn't even hear my prayers because I was not worthy. I distanced myself from God and stopped praying. What was the point? My friend is dead, and I'm not worthy. It all seemed pointless.

What Is That White Light?

Smoking cigarettes was my coping mechanism. It's how I coped with everything. I'd tell people at work when I was unwell, however, if I can get up to have a smoke, I can get up and go to work. I smoked when I was happy, I smoked when I was sad, and I smoked because I felt stressed. It was the same routine all the time. I'd get up, make a coffee and have a cigarette. I always had an allocated smoking area outside, and I never smoked inside our home.

It was a roller coaster ride. I'd always tried to give up and one time I gave up for three years but then something would happen. I was triggered by something from my past and I'd start up again. I didn't smoke through my pregnancies, but I remember when my son was about two months old having to call an ambulance because he was having a febral convulsion. I'd never seen anyone have an epileptic fit before. My baby, at two months old, had his eyes rolling backwards and his lips turning blue while his body shaked uncontrollably. I only remember the ambulance operator saying to put him on his side and make sure he wasn't near anywhere he could hurt himself. Smoking returned that day; it helped me to breathe deeper and breathe calmer. I felt like I could be a calmer mother by smoking. It definitely suppressed all my past hurt.

I remembered reading a book one time by a man named Allen Carr. He wrote about how he smoked 100 cigarettes a day. I didn't smoke that many, but he wrote that you should smoke while reading his book. He started chapters by saying if you are not currently smoking a cigarette then light one up before reading this chapter. I enjoyed reading his book but then I found a lot of people had stopped smoking after they finished the book. I never read the last chapter because I wasn't ready to quit.

After my prayers weren't answered and my friend died, I coped by smoking more cigarettes. One day out of desperation while I was home alone still thinking about my friend who died, I spoke out loud to say a prayer because I felt ashamed. I kept thinking, my friend died because of me. I was a dirty person who wasn't good enough for God to hear my prayer and

I said, "God if you can hear me. I promise, I'll stop smoking when this packet of cigarettes is finished. I'll try and be a good person from now on so you can listen to my prayers." That was it, that's all I said. I sat feeling proud of myself that I'd finally made the decision to quit smoking. It felt safe too knowing that I'd purchased a 50 pack of cigarettes because I now had a few days to relax, drink coffee and smoke.

I started marking my packet of cigarettes, so I knew how many were left. I thought to myself that with each one, whether I definitely needed to have it or not but who was I kidding, I was addicted to them and always told myself a reason why it was ok to have a cigarette. A few days passed, and it was late at night. Everyone else in my home was asleep. I'd cleaned the kitchen, made a coffee and sat outside to have a cigarette. I opened my 50 pack of cigarettes to see there was only two left. I enjoyed the first cigarette feeling normal as I sipped my coffee. I flicked through a news article I was reading on my phone and opened my packet of cigarettes to have my last smoke. It was like a funeral service having that last cigarette. I didn't cry but I wondered how I was going to cope tomorrow at work. I knew it was going to be a busy day, but it was ok because I was trying to get myself right with God. I was going to be so clean that God couldn't help but notice me the next time I prayed. I put the final cigarette out, went inside and worried about what tomorrow would be like.

The next morning, I got up. "No, I can't drink coffee," I thought to myself. "Otherwise I'll be looking for a cigarette." I made a cup of tea; it was terrible, but I wasn't looking for a cigarette at least. Later that morning my boss rang to ask for help on something important. They needed it as soon as possible, but no one knew how to extract the data from the system for the results. Another staff member rang about a problem with a supplier. A sales representative called to see if I had archived images of one of our products in a particular format. I'd only been working for an hour. How was this possible with everything happening all at once? It was all before I even had a chance to do my own work. I sat back in my chair and tried to breathe deeply and breathe calmly but it didn't work. I got up from my desk at home and drove to the local shops. I bought myself a packet of cigarettes and went home.

I put the kettle on; it was time for a coffee!!! I unwrapped the cigarette packet and opened the back sliding glass door to go outside. I sat staring at the packet of smokes for a little while, then realized how I couldn't cope with today at work if I didn't have one. I lit my cigarette and in the corner of my eye, I saw a person, but they were like a white light. The white light moved across the room, inside my house but when I got up to look at it, it was gone. I was standing outside my glass door, looking inside my house holding my cigarette, I was the only one at home then I heard an audible voice say, "Your words mean nothing." I instantly freaked out and thought to myself, "God is that you?" But I heard nothing else. I didn't know what to do. I realized in that moment a few things. God was real, I wasn't worth it, I'd lied to God and now my actions were unforgivable. I was angry that God didn't think I was worthy, so I distanced myself from God.

Not My Son, Please Help Me

Our baby girl was asleep; we'd finally got her into a good day time routine. I was busy doing laundry while she slept when it suddenly dawned on me. Today was the anniversary of my Grandpa's death. I dropped the clothes I was folding on the floor and started to weep. I'd nearly missed remembering the anniversary of his death. I felt ashamed that I'd been so busy that I almost forgot about it. I felt guilty that I hadn't paid any special attention to the day, I felt useless. Quietly I whispered, "Why God? Is this day always going to be a day of sadness for me? Why can't it ever be a day of celebration? Why God?" Then I just sat at the edge of the bed crying quietly so I didn't wake my baby girl from her day sleep.

A few years went past and I was pregnant again. Our three-year-old daughter was desperate for a baby sister. We asked her what about if it's a baby brother, but she shook her head and said she wanted either a baby sister or a puppy. We tried to hide the pregnancy initially until at least eight weeks before saying anything but our daughter made an announcement at her day care centre that mummy had been vomiting because the baby in her tummy was kicking all the food back up.

The time passed so quickly and before we were ready for it, I was now nine months pregnant and being told by my obstetrician to go straight to hospital as my waters had started to leak. It wasn't broken yet, but my obstetrician told me to go straight to hospital. Whether I was ready or not, this baby was determined to be born within the next 24 hours.

"It's a boy," the midwife announced, and we were overjoyed. Our daughter on the other hand was unimpressed that she didn't have a baby sister, but we told her that her baby brother brought a gift for her as she was now a big sister, so she happily agreed to meet her new baby brother. She looked at him as he slept and said, "Hello baby brother. I'm your big sister and I love you."

That night, my first night in hospital with my new baby boy, I realized that today was my Grandpa's anniversary. My son had been born on the anniversary of my Grandpa's death. I quietly wept happy tears as my baby boy slept.

My son had a good childhood. He was loving, kind, a little cheeky, but would always appear randomly at odd times to just give his Dad or me a hug and tell us he loved us.

My husband and I made every effort to have a happy home for our kids. We gave them everything their little hearts desired. Camping holidays, overseas vacations, every toy they ever wanted. Nothing was too much for our little darlins. If they wanted a birthday party, I was always triggered by what happened to me on my 13th birthday and would make every effort to do more than what they'd ask for. For our son's 10th birthday, we flew nine hours to take him to Hawaii as a surprise family holiday, but all he actually wanted was to have a small birthday party with friends back home. After a week, we flew back home, and I organized two birthday parties for him with different friends at each party. I knew it was too much, but I never wanted my own children to be upset about missing out on a birthday party.

As the years progressed, it was hard to believe my baby boy was going to be 15 soon. He didn't want a birthday party, but I wanted to help him celebrate. It was the anniversary of my Grandpa's death, and I loved that because of my son; it was no longer a day of mourning but a day of celebration. I became frustrated on why he didn't want to celebrate his birthday, but he'd become a little bit of a recluse. Getting him up for school became difficult as gaming had taken over his life. He started gaming all night playing online video games and was too tired for school in the morning. He stopped listening to both his father and me. His big sister was the only one he occasionally talked to but when it came time to spend time together as a family, he was either their grunting at us and not wanting to talk to us or was a no show. He only ate, slept and gamed in his room. If he went to school, I'd often get a call from the sick bay nurse to say he was unwell and they'd ask me to come and pick him up. He would come in the door at home and go to bed, so he was ready at 11pm to start gaming again.

Over the next five years, our relationship as mother and son soured but it wasn't just me. He stopped talking to his sister, he was rude to his father and gaming became his life. In those years we sought professional help for him through doctors, psychiatrists and psychologists. We refused initially for him to be put on happy pills because I couldn't understand what he could be sad about. However, in the end, we had no choice but to give in after three years of declining the pills, because he was now out of control and kept telling us he was depressed and it was the only solution. He took those happy pills only for a few days, said it made him feel numb then stopped taking them altogether. The arguments at home got worse and every now and again I'd see a slight hint of my loving baby boy but then he'd pick up his gaming remote, close his bedroom door and we only knew he was home when he started screaming into his headset of his video game to his other team players online or scream at us that our home internet was lagging.

I was worried about our son. I didn't approve of his girlfriend, and I didn't approve of his gaming, and no one was able to help my son as he stopped listening to all of us years ago. He now labelled himself as depressed and started talking about suicide.

One day, after he'd finished high school and got himself a job, he brought home a friend. It was a boy he'd gone to primary school with. I thought it was great that he had finally accepted a real friend into his life instead of just his online friends. My son stopped gaming but instead now he'd started smoking weed. His addiction to marijuana cost him half his pay and it made him happy, sad, angry and not pleasant to be around. My son and his old school friend started writing songs together. They spent a lot of time just smoking, writing and singing songs together. His father, sister and I walked on eggshells around him not knowing what to do. I'd tried being a supportive parent, an angry parent, and an eggshell parent where I said nothing that would make him sad. We tried all approaches, but nothing worked. We'd give him an inch and he'd take a mile. I started reading about how to cope living with a narcissist. We continued taking him to doctors, psychiatrists and psychologists but nothing worked.

One day, I was working from home while my nearly 20-year-old son and his friend were home. He asked if I wanted to listen to his latest song before he released it on spotify. He said, "I want you to be honest. Don't worry if you think it's bad or not, I just want to know the truth." So I sat with him as we each smoked a cigarette and listened to his song. It was an upbeat song, but I didn't like it. He looked at me as the song ended and asked what I thought.

I was honest. "It's good but your voice sounds a little off. Singing lessons would definitely help."

My son looked enraged in that moment. "What do you mean?" he shouted.

I replied, "You said for me to be honest so I'm being honest."

He stood up and screamed, "This is why I don't want to talk to you, because you make me so depressed. You are the reason I've been contemplating suicide as my 21st birthday present to all of you."

I stood silent for a moment. What had I done? Should I apologize and be the nice mum? Should I scream back at him and be the angry mum? I didn't know what to do. I stood up and looked at him and the quote from the movie Shawshank Redemption came to mind and I said, "Mate, we've done everything for you and you still resent us. We've been nice to you when you didn't deserve it, but it only made things worse. We've tried to discipline you for the times you scream at us, but it never helped the situation. You talk about suicide as a way to always get us to back off but I'm sick of it. Get busy living or get busy dying. Let me know when it's happening as I'm sick of walking on eggshells around you." I turned and walked off angrily, his behavior was too much; I didn't know how to help him anymore.

I heard my son's friend say, "I can't believe what your Mum just said." I was over it, what do I do? I walked inside our home to go back to work. That night I started to pray,

"Dear God, if you're real can you please save my son."

That was it, every night I said the same prayer for weeks when everyone else had gone to bed. I was used to being a nightowl. I'd then just sit and cry because I didn't know how to save my son. I didn't know if a prayer would help or not but I'd remembered how I'd last spoken to God briefly about my Grandpa's death anniversary and how I'd hoped that one day it would be a day of celebration - it ended up being the day my son was born. Was God real? Was it just all just a coincidence? I wondered to myself, in silence about the day my son was born, the same day as my Grandpa's death anniversary. I wasn't sure but because we'd tried everything else, this is the only hope I had left.

A few weeks went by, and my son announced, because of encouragement from his Dad, he'd searched and found himself a singing teacher who taught not far from our home. I was a little annoyed that I'd said it first, but my son and my relationship had now turned into a side way glance at each other. If I spoke to him, he was offended. If he spoke to me, I disliked his tone and we would always end up arguing, so we said nothing most days. In that moment I thought, our son had turned to his Dad for advice, it made me happy that at least he still listened to his Dad. My son continued to smoke copious amounts of marijuana and my son and I continued to fight but every night when everyone else was asleep, I'd pray the same prayer as before,

"Dear God, if you're real can you please save my son."

A few months had passed since I said the same prayer each night, and my son started showing up more. He didn't really speak to us, but he was present and joked around with his Dad and sister on occasion, or was just quiet in his bedroom. Gaming had definitely stopped but I didn't know what was going on. He said that for the last few months, he'd been going to singing lessons. Most times he was high on marijuana and one day his singing teacher said to him, "Do you mind if I pray over you?" He remembered agreeing to her because he thought to himself that famous musicians he followed thanked God in their award speeches. Prayer really didn't mean anything because he was an atheist but maybe it would help his singing career to take off.

My son started meeting up with people from a Christian home church community. Did my son join a cult? I wondered, but he seemed happier, so I didn't say anything.

Within six months our son invited his Dad and I to his water baptism. We went, not knowing what to think. My husband was more relaxed than me because he finally had his son back. Our son had stopped taking all those drugs a few months earlier, he was happy, he smiled often and he started showing up to most family dinners now instead of locking himself away in his bedroom. The times he wasn't with us, he was either working or spending time with other young men his age talking about their love for God together. During his water baptism, he gave what he called his testimony, explaining how different parts of his childhood were triggered by us, his parents, and in particular me. He explained in his testimony how he went from denying God to loving God. It was about a relationship with God not a religion. How the truth in the bible and encouragement from this community had helped Him see God was real. They showed Him and all the triggers he had for depression, thoughts of suicide, anxiety, drugs and thinking everyone, including his parents, hated Him, were lies. This was because he found, through the bible, prayer and this home church community that his parents did love him, and he didn't need drugs to be happy. He said that God took all those thoughts of depression and anxiety away from him because he only felt happy now.

I looked at my son, yes, he was happy, and as a parent I was very relieved. I didn't understand all those happy clappers at this home church, but I was happy for him. They were all nice people, but I kept an eye on them during my son's water baptism. Why were they all so happy? They were all different ages. It seemed odd watching a teenager or a young man talk so openly about their life to a non-relative at this home church. Why were they so relaxed? Why did they all smile and hug each other? Yes, I thought to myself, this must be a cult. I whispered my concern to my husband, but my husband only saw a room full of people who had helped our son. He was no longer a drug induced gaming addict who always talked about suicide - he had now changed. Our son was one way and now he was totally different. I was offended by most things my son had said in his testimony, and I wanted to leave sooner rather than later. Food was put on the table for everyone to share as a morning tea together after his water baptism, but maybe they laced it with some sort of drug? I thought that I was smarter than them, so I didn't eat the food offered.

Before his 21st birthday our son announced that he was moving out with a few of the boys from his home church community. We helped him move he only wanted his bed and told us everything else could be thrown out, he didn't want any of it. He looked at me and said, "Mamma, don't look at anything, just throw it all out." I smiled and hugged my son. I didn't say I would but I knew what I was going to do; I was about to go through everything in my son's old room. I was going to be putting my Sherlock Holmes' cap on before removing anything from his old bedroom. I thought to myself, what would he do if he realised a few months later that he needed something, but I'd thrown it out? No, I was taking care of everything. I'd go through it all myself.

The next day, I started the deep clean of my son's old bedroom. Garbage bags were being filled up so quickly. I went through every drawer in his desk to make sure I didn't throw out something he might want later on. He'd moved so quickly. It seemed like he said, "I'm thinking of moving out," to actually moving out in a few days but it had been a few weeks, maybe even a month or so.

As I was sorting through his old belongings, I came upon an envelope labelled 'to my family'; it had a covering note and also contained a note for each of us. One was labelled to me, another to his father and the last one to his sister. Before I started reading the covering letter, I thought to myself as I smiled, he knew I would go through his room. He must have wanted me to find these notes. As I started reading the covering letter, I realized it wasn't a loving note for us at all. It was his handwritten plan on how he was going to commit suicide as his gift to us for his 21st birthday. I couldn't read anymore. I sat in silence crying. Then I realized, my son had been planning suicide, but God saved my son. Through tears of an unbelieving mother who always prayed, "God if you're real, please save my son." God had saved my son.

CHAPTER 5

THE HEALING BEGINS

The Death Of Angry Ange

My son had moved out. He was 21 and living with people from the home church he went to. He was different because now he was always happy. Was he secretly on something? I thought, but I never saw him take any more drugs, so I continued to ponder on it while I sat smoking a cigarette.

He came back home every week to share a meal with us. I loved seeing him, but he always came over with his bible. Was this kid trying to get me to join a cult? I thought to myself. No way, I was smarter than that, I wasn't born yesterday. Who was this kid kidding? He couldn't fool me. He'd asked me about my prayer life, and I told him it was personal. He asked me if I was still reading my bible and because he kept asking about it each week, I had gone back to reading Genesis. He said that I should start from Matthew, it's in the New Testament. I shook my head, as I knew better. You don't start a book from the middle. What was this kid on about? I thought. He asked me about Jesus, and I had to ask him why he would talk about Jesus. Wasn't he the guy who died thousands of years ago on a cross? I remembered this Jesus was the one on the cross at the front altar at church from my old Catholic school days. Why was my son bringing him up? He told me Jesus was the answer. I just nodded as he talked, this kid knew nothing about life, yet he was so adamant about Jesus.

He tried quoting scripture to me but it all seemed like nonsense. It was totally irrelevant, even though he kept saying it was relevant, but what did my son know? I had a bible on my bedside table for over 20 years. I didn't read it but it was there. I don't know why it was there, but it always was. I wore a cross necklace sometimes; it was a nice piece of jewellery, and it had fake diamonds on it but I mostly wore it because it looked good on me and it was fashionable. Every now and again I'd open the bible, read the words, "In the beginning," then read something about this person begat this person. I couldn't really understand it, so I'd always put it down and go to do other things.

As my son spoke about Jesus, I thought, "Hang on, I'm the parent, don't come round here trying to tell me what to do because I'm your mother." I started to feel defensive against my own son. I couldn't understand why, but he was totally frustrating me. It happened every time he visited until one night I'd had enough and told him to stop trying to preach to me. "I'm not interested, I'm fine." Then anger built up in me every time he brought it up. I loved my son. However, why did he keep talking about God or this Jesus character all the time?

I started timing my son's visits, just like I did at that car dealership all those years ago. I'd give my son the benefit of the doubt and just allow him to talk about whatever he wanted. If he brought up God or Jesus, I'd let him talk for 10 minutes, then I'd make an excuse to leave the room. This happened for months. My husband and daughter knew how I felt and they did the same although they weren't as blunt as me.

One night, my son came around he had a bible in his bag, I could see it, but it didn't come out of his bag. He just put his bag down on the lounge and sat and spoke to us about his week at work. We all sat and listened as he talked about having prayer nights at his home. I watched him talk about others and he told us how happy he was. It made me think about how many years I'd lost my son to gaming, to addiction and it felt like my 21-year-old son was that sweet little 10-year-old who use to give random hugs and always tell me he loved me.

When my son was little, maybe four, even at 10 and still at 20, he always thought he was in the right. I'd always ask him to apologize and he always became defensive about it. "Why?" he'd always scream at me. Why did he have to apologize when he didn't think he was in the wrong. We'd talk about it when he was younger about why it was not a good choice to be mean to someone or why lying wasn't good and he would always reluctantly apologize. When he was older, making him apologize always ended in screaming, he'd end up apologizing and say sorry, but then he'd go off to his room and slam his bedroom door closed. I knew he hated apologising when he did something wrong, but I never said anything to anyone about it. I always kept that thought to myself. At least he ended up apologizing when he was in the wrong. It was good for him to know when he was in the wrong.

I started looking forward to my son's visits, mainly because he stopped pulling out his bible every time he came over. He seemed to have matured while he lived away from us. He'd gone back to calling me Mumma and I loved it. One particular night my son asked me a question - it was something about the bible and I told him to back off. I walked outside to have a cigarette and calm down and he watched me walk outside. As I sat outside, I looked through the large window from our back deck to the loungeroom and saw Him laughing and talking to his Dad. I sat smoking my cigarette, only noticing in that moment how happy our family was now.

A little time passed and my son opened the back sliding door and came out to see me. He looked at me and said, "Mamma, can I talk to you?" I nodded and he said, "I just went to the toilet and I quickly prayed and asked Jesus for help. I asked him to tell me how I could explain to you that you're wrong and I'm right from when we spoke before, but Jesus asked me to apologize to you because I'm wrong, I shouldn't have spoken to you the way I did. Mamma, I'm sorry. Can you please forgive me?"

I didn't know what to say in that moment. The first thing that crossed my mind was my son prayed in the toilet. Then I wondered why he was apologizing. I got up and hugged my boy, my beautiful baby boy. Even though he was a lot taller than I was, he bent down to hug me. He told me he loved me, and I told him I loved Him too. Then he went inside saying goodbye to his Dad and sister before he drove back to his new home.

That night, I sat quietly while everyone else went to bed. I couldn't understand how this happened, because it was so out of character for my son. For the first time ever, my son apologized to me. I was definitely in the wrong this time, but he apologised so easily. No door was slammed, no shouting from him, he just apologized, even though we both knew I was in the wrong. Who was this Jesus who my son prayed to? Ok, Jesus was important to my son. So, I decided that, even though it was a hard read, from tomorrow I'd go back to reading my bible to find the stories about Jesus in Genesis. God seemed real because he saved my son. I had to work out a way to get on God's good side. My grandparents were good people, so they must be in heaven. I had to start doing better.

My son started asking me about talking to people from his home church. Initially I said that I wouldn't for months but eventually as I watched how different and happy my son was now, I wondered why? Why was he so adamant for me to meet people from his home church? My son said, "Mamma, you and I are very close, I love you but I've been praying about you for a while now. The Lord told me that you refuse to be honest with me about some things because you don't want to share truths from your past with me because I'm your son and because you don't want to upset me." I nodded; he was right. I knew he was right because I didn't want him to know how broken his mother was. I thought about how a lot of my past was going to stay hidden; I couldn't talk about it because I didn't want my children or family to know the painful memories I had. "Okay," I replied, as I hugged my son; I trusted my baby boy. He said he'd organize it in the next few days.

A few days went past, and my son turned up at our home to take me to see a couple from his home church group. Who were these people? I thought, but my son said they were people who were older than me. My son reassured me that I'd feel more comfortable talking to them and how they'd walked with the Lord for over 40 years. They could help me, he told me. My son reminded me that it's just coffee and not to overthink it. My son's car left our driveway and as he drove out, I looked at the neighbor's house across the street. It felt different. Was that house that had stood there as our neighbor's home for over 20 years about to change or was it me? I wondered about it as my son drove.

I was a little apprehensive about the coffee. I wondered whether this husband-and-wife duo would bring out the bible and start quoting to me, but they didn't. I thought maybe they'd do a sermon like the priests do in a Catholic church, but they didn't. I thought maybe they'd make me confess my sins and then tell me what I could do to right all my wrongs, but they didn't. They just gave me coffee and asked me to tell them about myself.

I told them how I'd tried believing in God, but God didn't love me. I'd prayed to Him so many times, but He never heard me; He obviously thought I was too sinful to deal with. I'd tried everything to get God to hear me, but He never did so I either ignored Him or distanced myself from Him. I even prayed to the enemy one time when I didn't think God existed, but it was the thoughts of how those prayers each night helped my son. It was only something God could do. I had to give God credit for helping my son, I was never able to do those changes for him, myself. I told them how I changed my approach with God because of my son.

I was trying to have God in my life, so I started to avoid swearing, tried to be good to others, and read the bible. They asked why I was doing all of that. I thought, don't they get it? I'm trying to get to heaven because that's where my Grandparents are. The man from my son's home church said, "So, you've been trying to clean yourself up?"

I said, "Yes."

He said, "Only Jesus can clean you up."

I said, "I'm not worthy, I'm too filthy for Him to deal with."

He said, "The bible actually says to come as you are, you don't need to worry about cleaning yourself up. Jesus will do that in a way no one else can." I looked at this man like he was going to explain the tips on how to live a Godly life. I needed to know what I had to do to be accepted by God. For God to finally hear me and clean me up.

Then the man asked, "Do you believe in God?"

I said, "Yes." The answer came so quickly to me. I hadn't believed with all my heart before. If you'd asked me if I believed in God years ago, I would have said, "Not sure, maybe not." But now, I saw what He did for my son, and yes, I believe in God.

Then he said, "All you have to do is believe Jesus is the son of God, that He died on the cross to save you from all your past, present and future sins. God doesn't want you to stay away, He wants you to come to Him. If you believe that then you're saved and can go to heaven."

I said, "What do I have to do?"

He said, "Nothing. All you have to do is believe."

"That can't be right," I thought. "Well, I'm a pretty big sinner, if I look at the 10 commandments, I'd broken most of them."

He replied and said, "Jesus didn't come looking for the righteous, he came looking for us sinners and he wants a relationship with you." No, it couldn't be that easy. God wants a relationship with me but I'm a broken sinner who smokes cigarettes to suppress past hurt. How could He want a relationship with me? I wondered, as I urgently tried to search for an answer.

As he continued talking to me, my mind wondered off. I have no idea what he was saying next. I wondered to myself, if that was it. It can't be. Surely there's more to it. I knew from the decades of when I was a Catholic, I knew the rules. who was this man kidding? I wasn't born yesterday. The rules of being a Catholic included me doing good works for God to see me. Turning up to church, or at the very least, saying the Our Father Prayer, so God knew I was there.

When I was a Seventh Day Adventist, it included me not eating certain foods, and they were the only rules I really understood. All the other rules I hadn't made sense of, yet this man made it sound so simple. How could it be so simple? It can't be that simple. What was this man saying? Just say a pray to say I believe in Jesus is all I had to do? I thought God was unobtainable to me but in that moment, it was like all the barriers on why God didn't want me, was gone. My mind was suddenly quiet, not one thought. This was the first time in my life that it was just quiet.

In my mind, I started to pray and said, "God, if you can hear me, I believe in Jesus. I believe Jesus died on the cross to save me from my sins."

I sat looking at the man and woman sitting opposite me in their home but not seeing them. They looked at me and I said nothing. At that moment it was like a light bulb had just been turned on inside me. What was happening to me? I felt happy, and I didn't know why. Then I felt warmth, and I looked to the right and saw the sunshine. I shifted in my seat to get out of the sun and move into the shade, but I still felt this strange warmth all over my body. I felt my inside was like an explosion of happiness, every bit of grief, sadness, worries and anger I had was gone. It was amazing. What was this feeling? I thought as I sat still. What was this elation and joy? I felt so happy.

The only way I can explain it is that it felt like I was at a sold-out rock concert. You make your way to the merchandise stand to buy something, like a small piece of memorabilia to show I tried to get into the concert, but it was sold out - I wasn't good enough to get a ticket. Then the lead singer at the concert taps you on the shoulder and when you turn around the lead singer is looking at you, it's Jesus, and He's inviting you to come with Him. For me that was my first feeling of meeting the Lord and His Holy Spirit, I loved it. That feeling of love is nothing like I can compare to, it was nothing I'd ever felt before, not even with my Grandpa who I'd loved with all my heart. Imagine having not one worry, only feeling love, only feeling happiness. Not sure what changed on the outside at that moment, but my inside was alive as I sat in silence looking at the man and woman. The man smiled and said, "What your feeling is not even 10% of the love the Lord has for you." My whole body felt alive especially my mouth. For a moment I was speechless. I thought, I needed this guy's number, my husband was about to be so excited with a speechless wife. Then I couldn't stop talking, I was so excited. As my son drove me home, he just laughed and he couldn't say anything as I was so full of excitement and wouldn't stop talking. He drove me into our driveway, the house across the road was still there, it still looked the same but I felt different.

Later that night at home, I thought how I always used to think I wasn't born yesterday. No one could fool me but in reality, I was today zero days old when I realized God was real.

Angry Ange was dead. I couldn't explain it. I was just no longer angry like I use to be. It was like God had given me a new heart. I understand now that not everyone feels the exact same way (as I did) when God entered my life. Others who are thinkers start to question everything, until one day, instead of questioning everything they just realize the bible is God's truth. I'm a feeler and I now feel amazing. God sees me, He knows my name and I love the Lord. He saved me just like He saved my son. The change happened in an instant and the healing started from the inside. Some people find God through a religious organization and I'm happy for them, but for me, God met me where I was because religion failed me. He pulled me from the muck and the mire of where I was in my life and transformed me into a better version of me. A version that didn't include me being angry with the world anymore.

CHAPTER 6

CRAZY GOD STORIES

The Enemy Attack

My son asked me one day, not long after I realized God was real, if I'd prayed and asked Jesus to forgive my sins and invite Jesus to come into my life. "No, I told him, I pray to God." He started reading scripture to me to prove his point (Acts 4:11-12, John 14:6, Romans 5:1 and Romans 3:23-25), which confirmed only through Jesus could we be made right with God. I thought about what he said and after a few weeks I prayed to God for guidance while I was doing some chores around our home. My husband was also helping out but he mostly did the outside cleaning, while I cleaned inside the house. In my mind as I dusted a shelf I said,

> "Dear God, I want to ask you something. I've been thinking about what my son said about praying and asking Jesus to forgive my sins and come into my life. I'm sorry God if it's not right because I only understand to pray to you. If you think it's okay then I want to do it one day, but I'll need exactly 10 minutes to pray about it, and I want to be on

> my knees to pray. I only want to pray to Jesus when I'm home alone. In Jesus name, Amen."

As soon as I said Amen, my husband walked in and said he was going to the corner store; he just remembered something he needed. He said he would be gone at least 10 minutes and wanted to know if I needed anything. I shook my head in disbelief as he never just popped down to the corner store; he'd never told me in the past how long he'd be gone for. My mind started racing, I didn't have time to think of what to say to Jesus, I just had to do it now. I heard my husband's car leave our driveway. I put my dusting cloth to the side and got down on my knees on the floor in our dining room.

"Hi Jesus, I'm sorry we haven't spoken before. I've only just found out to pray to you. I'm a sinful person and have done a lot wrong. I can't name them all because there are too many. Can you please forgive me for all my many sins. Please come into my life. In Jesus name, Amen."

I continued to sit on the floor after saying my short prayer and cried. I don't know why I was crying. Maybe it was because I realized in that moment how sinful I was. If I looked at the 10 commandments, I knew I broke most of them. After some time of just crying, I wiped my face, composed myself, and as I got up again to continue cleaning, my husband walked in. Somehow, he couldn't tell I'd been crying and we continued our day like normal.

That night, I went to bed but it was such a disturbing sleep. I kept having nightmares that were so scary I didn't know what to do. I kept trying to say the Our Father Prayer for the demonic dream to stop but it didn't work. I woke up the next morning and had copious amounts of coffee to get through my day. That second night I went to bed and it started again. The same demonic dream as the night before. I tried to say the Our Father prayer, but I kept forgetting the words and having to restart because of fear from the dream, but the dream continued. It was another restless night of no sleep. By the third morning I was exhausted. I could barely keep my eyes open, but I was too scared to sleep. I thought of a plan, I would stay up for as long as I could and only go to bed when I was totally exhausted. That third night I went to bed and the same demonic dream happened again. I saw dark figures so black trying to claw at me; I felt like they were attacking me. Every time I closed my eyes the dream continued. I couldn't sleep but I couldn't stay awake; I was exhausted and continued to try and say the Our Father prayer but kept forgetting the words. I restarted the Our Father prayer but everytime I closed my eyes the visions I saw were scarier than before.

On the morning of the fourth day, I knew my son was coming to visit. I would ask him about it as I continued to drink more coffees than normal. I couldn't put two words together properly. I couldn't function on such minimal sleep. I didn't understand why I hadn't called my son earlier when this all started happening but maybe it was because he also worked and I didn't want to trouble Him. I wanted my son to pray for me. When my son arrived, I told Him what had happened, but he said, "Mamma, why haven't you asked Jesus for help?" I thought to myself, I don't know. My son continued, "Jesus is a powerful name when the enemy attacks. Just ask Him for help instead of relying on your own strength."

That fourth night I went to bed and I saw the images and figures of things from my dream in my bedroom. I touched my face, yes, I was still awake, I hadn't even got into bed, yet the dream was now happening in my room. I jumped under the covers and tried to pray the Our Father prayer. Finally, I was able to say all the words of the prayer. I opened my eyes, nothing was in my room but as I closed my eyes, they were back in my dream, even though I was still wide awake. I remembered feeling fearful for my life but then what my son had said came to mind about Jesus, so in my mind I said, "Jesus, please help me," and it stopped!! The nightmare dreams I'd been having for the last four nights just stopped. I sat up in bed, so appreciative for what Jesus had just done for me. I realized too that in the last four days, I hadn't read my bible. I'd spent no time in prayer yet when I called on Jesus for help, he was right there to help me. I laid down in bed and instantly fell asleep to the best night's sleep I'd had in a long time.

One night, a year after that first attack from the enemy, I went to sleep and the same dream was back but I was more secure in my faith - I had confidence in Jesus. I knew now that I was a child of God. As the dream started, I sat up and said, "I'm a child of God, because of the authority from Jesus, I'm telling you to get out, in Jesus' name. I laid back down and had a peaceful night's sleep.

Stubborn v's Surrender

I'm stubborn, I've been that way for a long time. Maybe I wasn't stubborn to begin with but because of my childhood and life experiences, I grew to be a stubborn adult.

I'd found God through people's encouragement for me. My son played a big part in it. Specifically in the the way God saved Him. The community of faith I now belonged to helped to keep me grounded. I felt comfortable asking others about their journeys - their testimonies on how God came into their life. They each told me their own stories, and they noted the importance of surrender. I didn't understand what they meant and being new to this Christian walk I didn't want to over complicate it for myself. I loved spending time with Jesus.

My son came to our home each week for a meal, and he started asking me about surrender. He said I needed to surrender myself to the Lord and asked if I'd done that. I told him I was fine but I'd do it in my own time. I wanted to better understand what surrender was. My son explained surrender is surrendering yourself to God, allowing Him to show you the way and to stop being stubborn. I told my son I'd think about it.

For the next two weeks I thought about it and then decided maybe I'd already surrendered, but I didn't know. When others at church asked me if I'd surrendered, I said, "Yes," because I thought I had. I wasn't really sure; it was nothing to focus on. I'd been reading my bible, and I spent time in prayer every day. The thoughts about surrender came to mind but I disregarded it often.

One night I went to bed and had a strange dream -

I was running along a wide path. There were people to my right but I couldn't see the end of where on my right because the road was so wide. There were people in front and people behind, but I couldn't see where the end was for any of us. My arms and legs were moving in a running motion. I thought I was in a race, I wasn't out of breath, and I felt fantastic. I must be in a marathon, and I'm not last because people were behind me. I'd never run a marathon before, and I felt proud of myself.

I looked to my left, I was running on the edge of a cliff, but I felt safe, I didn't for a moment think I'd fall off the side. My arms and legs continued to move in a running motion, and I was proud of how fit I was not to be out of breath during a marathon. As I looked past the cliff edge into the distance on my left, I saw a large bridge. It was a bridge of light, it had the colours of a rainbow but it wasn't arched, and it was a flat rainbow. On the right of the rainbow bridge was a black dirty chimney. It was tilted towards the bridge at a 45-degree angle. I continued to run and watch the bridge and chimney. I saw what looked like a person covered in draped material from head to toe in only black. I couldn't see any faces because I only saw from a side angle, but as they stepped onto the rainbow bridge, they turned white. I watched a few people appear with this black garment, step onto the rainbow bridge and turn white. They all walked along the rainbow bridge in single file, away from the chimney and then I couldn't see them anymore. As I was watching them, I saw a line stretch from the rainbow bridge to me. It was narrow, it had the rainbow colours on it, but I refused to step onto it. I was scared of heights, but I looked away and continued to run in the marathon I was in, still so proud of myself for having the stamina to run this marathon.

Looking to the front of the line I could now see the finish line. I tried to run faster so I could get a better placing for the race but my arms and legs were moving in the same rhythm as everyone else. No one sprinted past me and we all just ran together in formation. It seemed odd but I couldn't control it. As I got closer to the finish line, I realized it wasn't a finish line at all. We were all running to the edge of a cliff. I tried to scream for everyone to stop, to let them know we would all fall and die if we didn't stop. We all continued moving our arms and legs in the same rhythmic motion. No one else reacted in my dream to running to the cliff edge. I wondered how no one else I was running with could see what was happening, it was like they were all oblivious to the truth.

I was now almost at the front of the line. I saw far in the distance (more than 10 kilometres or six miles away) a soft patch of sand. I don't know how I knew it was soft, but I just did. I was now at the front of the line. I was falling to my death and beneath me were sharp edged rocks. I thought about how I'd learnt to sky dive on one of our cruises I'd been on. It was skydiving in a controlled environment in a tube, but the instructor taught us by just moving your hand a certain way or how your feet were positioned that you could control how you moved through the air. I tried it several times, but I was still just falling towards the sharp rocks. I closed my eyes, put my hands together as I prayed, "Jesus I surrender." I opened my eyes and found I was standing on the soft sand. I wasn't hurt.

The next day, I knew my son would be around; I'd wait and ask him about the dream to see if he could interpret it for me. I remembered everything so clearly from my dream. I wondered if it was somehow connected to my birth mother and started quietly freaking out about it. I'd never been so excited to see my son. I told him I'd had a strange dream, I asked him if I told him my dream whether he could interpret it for me, but he said, "No. Mamma, pray and ask the Lord to give you guidance on your dream." he told me how through prayer you can ask the Lord to give you scripture as clarification.

The next day I decided to go to my secret place, shut the door and pray in private.

> "Lord, it's me. I had a strange dream last night and it's quietly freaking me out. I don't know if it's a good dream or a bad dream. I spoke to my son, and he said to ask you for scripture as clarification."

Instantly, I started thinking of James 1, 17. I was annoyed with myself now because my own mind was making stuff up.

"Lord, any scripture please?"

Again, I thought of James 1,17. Why do I keep thinking of that? I thought, because there is no James in the bible. It was only Matthew, Mark, Luke, John then Acts. I hadn't read past Acts so I thought maybe James is in the Old Testament. I picked up my mobile and opened my digital bible app. I scrolled to Matthew, Mark, Luke, John then Acts. No James. I scrolled up to Genesis and looked for James but couldn't find it. Then, as I scrolled from Genesis back down to Matthew somehow my finger scroll became strong and the bible app went all the way towards Revelation. Suddenly I noticed it. James was a book in the bible, but I'd never seen it before. I opened it up to James 1, 17.

> James 1:17 NKJV [17] "Every good gift and every perfect gift is from above, and comes down from the father of lights, with whom there is no variation or shadow of turning."

My question to the Lord was - is it a good dream or a bad dream? This verse in scripture confirmed, it was good, the dream was from God. The Lord showed me the importance of surrender in a way I finally understood.

That was my first conversation with the Lord. He taught me about surrender when I was too stubborn to know the importance. I'm still surrendering things to Him now, but I've learnt to allow Him to show me what to focus on next instead of me trying to fix me. The purification process with the Lord takes time; I'm still a work in progress.

The Lord has tried to show me a few times now how I still go to my pantry or fridge daily to grab something to eat between meals because that is a trigger from my past of not always being able to have a meal, and it has stuck with me. I haven't surrendered it to Him yet so he can help me. The Lord is being patient about it. I'm being stubborn but I'm either a size S for small or a size XL for extra-large. My husband tells me he loves me all the time regardless of my shape and I'm unsure why I haven't allowed the Lord to work on that part of me yet. The Lord reminds me often that I don't need to be perfect because Jesus was already perfect for all of us. At the end of the day, we are all human. I'm also not late when I choose to do anything because I don't have to hurry things along because the Lord's timing is always perfect.

We get to choose which path to walk in life.

Through surrender to God, we walk a narrow path. If I surrendered to myself and my wants, needs and desires then I get to walk a wide path with so many others. Life gets busy and we don't know we are on a wide road with others to destruction. I chose to surrender to God because God's way is so much better than anything I could do myself.

> Matthew 7:13-14 NLT [13] "You can enter God's Kingdom only through the narrow gate. The highway to hell is broad, and its gate is wide for the many who choose that way. [14] But the gateway to life is very narrow and the road is difficult, and only a few ever find it."

Same verse but New King James Version. Both give the same context.

> Matthew 7:13-14 NKJV [13] "Enter by the narrow gate; for wide is the gate and broad is the way that leads to destruction, and there are many who go in by it. [14] Because narrow is the gate and difficult is the way which leads to life, and there are few who find it."

Slapped By A Moth

I was a new Christian. I'd just found out that God was real. I had Jesus in my life. The news was wonderful. I couldn't contain my joy. I wanted to tell everyone about it, but for the first time I'd noticed the words I'd been using. Every conversation previously included a swear word. If a swear word wasn't spoken, then the old angry Ange didn't know how to explain anything properly in a sentence, but it never bothered me before. I didn't try and stop swearing but it just sought of stopped. Every now and then at the start of my journey with the Lord, a swear word would pop out of my mouth so randomly but somehow I noticed it now when it happened and I didn't like it.

I was driving to work one day, and singing to my Christian songs, which was my new normal. I would have random conversations with the Lord. On one particular day, I asked the Lord to make me accountable for the way I spoke. I asked Him to specifically remind me about being respectful to others.

I arrived at work, and the long one-and-a-half-hour drive didn't seem so bad today. After a short period of time, I made a coffee and went to the smoker's area. It was located outside the main building under a small, roofed area, similar to a gazebo but with a metal roof. I stood smoking a cigarette and sipping my coffee.

Another staff member from the factory appeared. We smiled at each other as we'd worked for the same company for a while and greeted each other. He asked about one of the staff in the office and as I was about to say exactly what I thought of that person a large black moth nearly the size of my face appeared. It was flying towards me. I wondered for a moment if it was a bat, but it was a large moth. It came up to my face, and its wing gently swiped my lip. It didn't sting, there was no pain, the touch was as soft as a feather, but I heard a loud slap noise. For a moment I thought to myself that I must have imagined it. Then, the staff member I was talking to looked at me and said, "Did you just get slapped on the mouth by a moth?" Only then did I realize it was real and I hadn't imagined it. I nodded at the staff member and, in my mind, said, "Sorry Lord."

The staff member asked me again about someone in the office. I looked and saw the large black moth flying back towards my face. I said, "I don't really have anything to say about that person." The large moth turned in that moment and flew away, never to be seen again.

I learnt that morning to be mindful of my words. If you pray about something specific to God, He answers our prayers in his way not our way. It's always gentle and done with love.

In My Weakness, God Is Strong

> Romans 12:19 AMP [19] "Beloved, never avenge yourselves, but leave the way open for God's wrath [and His judicial righteousness]; for it is written [in Scripture], "Vengeance is Mine, I will repay," says the Lord." [Deut 32:35]

I was going on a seven-week vacation. My husband planned the trip, and I was excited for this new adventure. We'd never done anything like this before. Travelling through the Baltics then the Mediterranean on two seperate cruises! I was so excited but then I became worried about my work. What about my boss? How would the staff cope with me being away? I'd made myself so important at work over 15 years at my manufacturing job, I worried that they wouldn't cope without me.

I contacted my boss of the manufacturing company I worked for and spoke to Him about my husband's surprise. I asked if it was ok to have that much time off, and I told him about how worried I was about the jobs I did for work not getting done and he reassured me, it would be fine. He had a plan; he would get back to me. He was a good boss.

Several days passed and my boss notified me that I was to train one of the girls in the office and teach her some of my tasks so she could do it while I was away. If I did that for four months then I didn't have to worry. He was a good boss and had a great plan. Obediently, I drove the one and a half hours to work a few times a week to train this new staff member on how to do some parts of my job.

This new staff member was excellent; she was able to grasp most of the new things I taught her with ease, so I felt more relaxed knowing my work was going to be okay. That portion of my role was covered. I took a deep breath and spent time in prayer each night so grateful that everything was working out for my co-workers and my boss. I loved my boss; he sometimes reminded me of my Grandfather. He was caring, he was a family man, and he was important to me.

I was only a new Christian at that stage, and I'd play my newfound love of Christian songs in the car and drive the one and a half hours to work singing to the Lord like I was performing a concert for Him. When the speakers in my car started playing up, I just started turning the volume up, but each time I did, somehow the music became softer. I found when I turned the volume down, somehow, I could hear it better. "The Lord is cheeky like that," I thought. He was lovingly telling me that He loves me singing to Him but just not screaming at Him for 90 minutes through my car performances with the volume so loud.

My holiday was fast approaching. I only had three weeks to go before my seven-week holiday. I spoke to the staff member I'd been training to ask how she felt she was going and she informed me she was good. She didn't really need me anymore. That was great, how fantastic - she's so clever. I continued to perform other roles that this staff member had not been trained on. They were tasks my boss said could be done when I came back from holidays.

My boss rang while I was working from home - they had an urgent problem. One of our sales managers was leaving and they had no way to do the admin portion of her role. He asked me for help. I loved it when my boss ever called me for help. It made me feel needed and important. I needed historical data of the admininstration work this sales manager used to perform to help my boss with this new project.

In shock, I received over 20 separate spreadsheets of data. Each spreadsheet had multiple tabs of information going back over 10 years. The old salesperson apparently wasn't giving any real guidance before her last day. The accounts staff member who had been assisting that sales manager for over 10 years said she never performed the full reconciliation portion and couldn't help. All she did was wait for the sales manager's reconciliation, which confirmed percentages and values by state, so she knew how to apply the customer's payment to their account. She said she had no idea how to do the full reconciliation to split by state, by percentages or dollar value as she explained, her job was only to apply payments and process credit rebates where applicable. She sent through examples of what the exiting sales manager had sent her in the past to assist with this new project and I was grateful for her help. I was instructed by my boss that I needed to work out a way to fix it before I went away on my seven-week vacation.

I was overwhelmed when the emails of data were sent to me. How do I reconcile years of data, create a new efficient process then streamline it? So that the accounts staff member could continue her side of the payment allocation that was currently taking her three hours per transaction. I tried different methods of building spreadsheets but nothing worked. I stayed up till I was exhausted. Some nights this was 11pm and other nights I'd stop working at 1am in the morning. This happened for a week. I'd always start again at 5am in the morning but trying to build the data was impossible.

A few nights into the second week, it became too much. I didn't know what to do as everything I tried didn't work. I sat and cried in silence very late one night. Everyone else in my home was asleep, then a verse from scripture came to mind; it was something about how nothing was a problem for the

Lord. Then another verse from scripture popped to mind, "What's impossible for man is possible for God."

I prayed and asked the Lord for help. I had no idea how to do it. I'd tried it on my own for over a week, I felt useless. During my prayer I suddenly had an idea. I tried it and it worked. I prayed again to thank Jesus for his help, and without Him giving me that idea I would have continued to spiral into depths of despair and I would have failed my boss and other staff that this new reconciliation process would have affected.

The idea that night, the one I received from the Lord, meant the full reconciliation somehow now would only take 10 minutes a week moving forward, and the payment allocation instead of three hours would also only take 10 minutes per transaction. I tested it over several days. The timing was indeed 10 minutes for the full reconciliation and 10 minutes to reconcile the allocation of payment. The only time needed after that was to apply the payment into the system. I continued to praise the Lord as I summarized and built the historical data for my boss. I created reconciliations for the new weekly data for my boss. When it was finished, I again praised Jesus for His help in giving me such a brilliant idea on how to do it.

It was my final working day before holidays had arrived. Today, I was handing my work mobile to the staff member I'd trained for the last few months. I was presenting the updated reconciliation to my boss and staff member he chose to perform this new reconciliation process. The day went well; my boss was surprised at how three hours of work was now down to 10 minutes. It would no longer take days per customer for reconciliations to be done. It now only took 10 minutes for all customers. I couldn't tell my boss that it was because the Lord had helped me. My boss was an atheist and telling him about Jesus wasn't a good idea because he was offended at times just seeing my new cross necklace that I started wearing at work.

As I left and said farewell, I went to see my boss to hug him goodbye but he wasn't interested in saying goodbye. He didn't thank me for the work I'd done, that impossible task he'd given me. He just waved for me to get out of his office. I tried to tell him I was giving my work phone to the staff member I trained and how he had my personal mobile number if he needed anything, but he was having none of it and gestured for me to get out of his office. I went to my car, put my work laptop on the passenger seat and drove out of the work driveway and started to cry. I was in shock at my boss's rudeness. Not even a thank you or a nice goodbye! Just a hand gesture, a flick of his wrist to tell me to get out of his office. The old angry Ange would have told him to his face exactly what I thought but I couldn't anymore. God had given me a new heart. I still loved my boss, but I couldn't tell him directly how much he'd hurt me.

Instead of calling a friend to vent my frustration I knew only the Lord would understand, so I called out to the Lord like a speed dial from my heart. I didn't want to gossip but I needed to get past the hurt, the rejection, and my annoyance at being treated like a fool. I prayed and vented to the Lord for 30 minutes, crying and asking the Lord why were the efforts not appreciated, but no verse from scripture came to mind. I then started praying for my boss. I prayed that one day my boss would know that God was real, that the Lord loved him just like the Lord loved me because scripture says God has no favourites. I put my Christian worship music on and listened to it for the drive home. My personal phone rang, I didn't see who it was and didn't pick it up; I was still too upset to talk to anyone. The drive was longer tonight, there was so much traffic. It took me two hours to get home, and I was exhausted.

Pulling into my driveway at home, I looked at my personal phone. One of my friends from work had called. She said my boss was trying to reach me yet I looked and saw he hadn't rung my number. She explained that one and a half hours ago one of the main pieces of equipment at the factory had stopped working. It meant because of this one piece of equipment not working that the factory could only do at most 50% production. My boss would lose money if it wasn't rectified, but they had no way to fix it. The company that sold them the equipment confirmed it was out of warranty, but the repair cost was quoted as $22,500. They also confirmed a brand-new piece of this equipment would cost $25,000. My boss was trying to urgently organize for a new one at $25,000. He'd forgotten that I'd given my work phone to the staff member I'd trained. He'd either forgotten he had my personal mobile number or was too embarrassed to call me and ask for help after being so rude and that's why I got the call from a person at work who was a friend. I told my work friend I'd fix it. It would take 10 minutes and I'd phone my boss after to tell him it was done; she thanked me for the help. I went to my home office, plugged in my work laptop, completed the purchase and all documentation then called my boss to give him the update. He knew my personal number when I called but pretended he wasn't at all alarmed by the piece of equipment that had blown at the factory. He thanked me for my help, and he told me to have a wonderful holiday. I smiled as I hung up the call with my boss.

I prayed and thanked the Lord that through my weakness He could be strong for me. I thanked the Lord for changing my boss's heart about me going on a seven-week vacation. I thanked the Lord for the reminder that when He's quiet it doesn't mean the Lord's not listening but instead, He's preparing something for our good and His glory. I thanked the Lord that in my times of desperation when it all seemed impossible that nothing is impossible for God. The Lord always shows up, His love is eternal and all I have to do is be still so He can do the work in my life and in other people's lives so they can look back at the footsteps of Jesus in their own lives.

Jobless - Facing My Identity

Working for the same company for nearly 17 years was something I never really planned on doing. It was a handful of people who I worked with that kept me grounded. My boss was amazing but he was getting old. I was an average person who always feared being fired and not being able to provide for my family. I worked so the mortgage and bills could be paid. I gave money generously to others if I thought they couldn't afford something because I remembered a time when we counted coins to buy bread and milk.

The company that I worked for had been sold. The new owners wanted everyone but me. Old and new friends with whom I'd worked apparently asked the new owners for me to join the new business but were told, "No!! Angie is not part of our business plan moving forward." They all called initially to find out about passwords for my old files but then it all stopped.

I continued to work for my old boss for a few weeks to finalize everything for Him. I pretended to be happy, a new adventure I'd say, but I cried most of the time. A month after I stopped working my husband asked me why I was rushing around one Sunday night and I told Him because it would be a busy week at work coming up and I always got a call from my boss early in the week. My husband looked at me and said, "he's not calling you. You don't work for him anymore." I stood silent for a little while then went and smoked cigarettes to numb the hurt.

Another week passed and I told my husband that I thought our insurance or email had been hacked. He looked at me puzzled and asked me why I thought that. I laughed and said because I got an email saying the direct debit for payment of our insurance didn't go through. The email said it was due to insufficient funds. He asked me what funds I was expecting and I reminded him my wage of course. He held my hand and said, "You don't have a wage anymore. You're unemployed and not working. I ran back outside to smoke more cigarettes to numb the hurt. I knew I'd have to face reality eventually, but I wasn't ready yet.

I kept a brave face for my family and friends. "Yes, I'm good," I told everyone. Only a very small handful of people knew I wasn't. When my husband went to work each day, I did the housework, but when it was done, I just sat and self-loathed about my situation. I distracted myself by flicking through social media for hours. I had day sleeps, I binge watched TV series I hadn't seen before and then I stopped leaving the house. When my husband came home from work or one of the kids came to visit me, I was happy again. This roller coaster lasted for several months. During that time, my husband and I went on a holiday. It was a wonderful vacation, but when we came back home, nothing had changed. I was back to my reality and depths of despair.

I went to my home church each Sunday and I always felt alive, spending time with everyone. I loved the Lord and it filled me with so much joy each Sunday but by Monday I was back to feeling down but pretending to be positive. My pastor at church asked me how I was going. One day he asked me, "Have you figured it out yet?" I looked at him a little puzzled then smiled like I had everything figured out when really I didn't. The loss of my job had weighed heavily on me. I felt useless and like a failure. How does a company get sold, and out of 30 people, they only want 29? Or out of 40 people, they only want 39. The common factor in both was me. I was the one they didn't want. It really hurt. I wondered if it was because I told everyone I was now a Christian. I wondered if it was because most people I worked with, including my boss, were atheists and that was the issue. It didn't matter. I was jobless and their lives went on like before but mine was now very different.

One night after several months, I decided to go back to my secret place. Exactly what it says in scripture:

> Matthew 6:6 NLT. "But when you pray, go away by yourself, shut the door behind you, and pray to your Father in private. Then your Father, who sees everything, will reward you."

To be honest, I hadn't spent any time in my secret place for a few months while I self-loathed about my situation. "Why was I such a reject?" I thought constantly. Through random prayer times, I found joy. Through time in scripture, I found peace and through my community at my home church I found clarity for things I'd missed. I had been so upset about losing my job that I didn't realize the blessing. The Lord had separated me from my old identity. The Lord was giving me time to spend time with Him so He could help me. The Lord had already provided a community of faith for me, they were wonderful and I constantly sought their encouragement, guidance and love during those times.

During that time, I learnt:

1. I had actively sought any distraction so I didn't have to face anything head on, but in reality, the Lord had been patiently waiting to have a conversation for my season.
2. I had feared rejection because I needed others to like me. I was better now, no longer angry Ange but I feared rejection because my birth mother had rejected me as a child.
3. I felt useless but really the Lord was showing me I was useful and all I had to do was surrender to His will not mine.

4. I felt like everyone at my old work hated me but it didn't matter what they thought because without the Lord they are all broken people living in a broken world.
5. I felt used - all that effort for nearly 17 years. All that time spent negotiating with suppliers, building relationships for a better future, creating and streamlining processes. It all felt like such a waste of time for my future. However, working for a manufacturing company until retirement wasn't part of the Lord's plan for me.
6. I felt like everyone had lied to me but I was the one clinging to something that wasn't meant for me. I found truth in scripture to set myself free from all the lies that I'd been telling myself. The condemning thoughts I had, that God didn't love me anymore because I was a failure were more lies. The truth is, if a thought contradicts scripture, then the thought is not from God.
7. I felt hurt that no one from my old work really cared about me. They didn't reach out to see if I was okay but they are as much in the dark about life as what I used to be before the Lord came into my life.
8. I was worried about my finances however, it somehow had a strange way of working out. We've still been able to pay the mortgage and put food on the table.
9. I was the one no one wanted but Jesus reminded me that He left the 99 for me.

The blessing of being separated from what I once knew was painful but when the Creator of the universe is in charge, we know it's for our good. It's a time of growth; it's a time for us to face what we've been denying. It's a time for us to surrender and trust in God and His wonderful plans, for our lives.

Wasp Alert

It was Christmas Eve. I'd purchased all the gifts my husband and I had planned for the family. Everything was wrapped as I sat outside for hours listening to Christian worship music or flicking through social media as I smoked a cigarette. We were a great team; my husband and I were ready for Christmas.

My husband walked past me; he'd been downstairs in his man cave. It was an external room extension we'd done some years prior, below our top deck. The room was filled with the usual things you'd find in a small man cave; it had a few instruments, a pool table, a TV and a stereo. My husband played the guitar; he would spend time learning new songs or playing old songs he knew off by heart. Leaving his man cave, he walked towards the backyard stairs and along the gangway to where I was sitting on our outdoor lounge decking area. As he was walking past me, he kicked one leg in the air. I thought he wanted to do a random dance, so I quickly put my phone down and stood up to dance, but he said, "I've just been bitten on my ankle by a wasp." I ran to get some antiseptic cream for him.

The following morning, it was Christmas Day. We'd already prepared everything to go and see family for Christmas lunch so nothing else had to be done. My husband and I assumed our normal positions before the festivities began. He went back down to his man cave while I sat on the outdoor lounge; it was like a repeat of the day before. My husband walked past me and kicked his leg up in the air, just like the day before. I clapped and said, "I'd give that an 8 out of 10." He looked at me and asked what I was talking about. I said, "Were you re-enacting your leg kick from yesterday? I was scoring your thespian skills." He looked pained and pointed at his foot and said, "I've just been stung on my toe by a wasp." I ran to get more antiseptic cream for the same foot as the day before but this time it was for his toe. I asked, "How do you keep getting bitten when I've been out here for hours and not been stung once?" He shook his head in disbelief as I put the cream on his toe. "I know why I'm not getting bitten," I said, and he asked why. "I'm a child of God, Jesus protects me. I have the Lord in my life, so I don't need to worry," but my husband thought it was nonsense. I tried explaining to him how Jesus was real but all he could say was that he was going to go find the wasp nest. There had to be a nest somewhere. He was preparing to exterminate the wasp nest. "Found it!!" I heard him shout then he hobbled past me to go and prepare for the wasp nest annihilation.

My husband came out wearing several t-shirts, a large long-sleeved jumper, and a hoodie jumper where the hood was tied so tightly that you could only see his glasses. He wore a long pair of jeans that were apparently hiding other layers of undergarments, a long pair of socks over the jeans so the wasps couldn't get into his pants and Ugg boots. It was strange to see such an outfit at Christmas because where we live, Christmas is in summer not winter.

He held his can of bug spray and walked past me; he was on a mission. I stood upstairs, not far from the wasp nest as I watched my husband walk downstairs. He planned on spraying directly at the nest from underneath to make sure none could escape. I stood only a meter or two away from all the action as I watched my husband, the new wasp terminator. He positioned his can of bug spray. On the first press of the bug spray I heard a scream. It was my husband; he'd been bitten again, but this time on his arm by a rogue wasp. This only made him more determined. He sprayed for longer, directly at the nest and was bitten several more times on his arms but there was no telling Him to stop because he was adamant that he was terminating every wasp in the nest today.

One very large wasp flew towards me. It was at least 10 centimeters long. It looked chunky and it was about as thick as my thumb. It flew towards my face as I stood unprotected in any wasp terminator outfit. I closed my eyes to pray, and, in my mind, I spoke so fast, but I knew the Lord would be able to understand.

"Lord, it's me. I know I've been boasting for two days about not being bitten by a wasp but please protect me because I'm a child of God."

I opened my eyes and watched the wasp circle me. It was as though I wasn't there, and the wasp flew off. Thank goodness it flew off in the opposite direction to my husband!

Sunglass And Quiet

My husband and I were on another cruise. We unpacked the clothing from our suitcases and stored everything away in our cabin. We were ready to explore the cruise ship.

We went up to the top deck, there was a bar, there was a smoking area on one side and a non-smoking area on the other. We each ordered a drink and the barman told us he would deliver the drinks to us. My husband and I looked around the large area. It had lounge chairs everywhere, separated by small coffee tables and towards the back of the ship there were sun lounges.

I looked and saw two men facing the bar area towards the back of the ship, and smoking cigars. They had sunglasses on; they didn't talk to each other; they just sat staring off into the distance as they each puffed on their cigars with sunglasses on. I pointed to their table. "Let's sit there," I said.

My husband asked, "There are so many empty seats on both sides, why do you want to sit there?" I didn't know why I wanted to sit there either. I just knew that I'd had a water baptism the week before. I'd declared my love to God for everyone to know. Normally I wouldn't sit next to two ruthless looking characters but today I wanted to brighten their day and tell them about God because God was real and He loved everyone. My husband had no idea what I was up to; he followed me over reluctantly but he walked as though he was my bodyguard. I thought to myself, that I had Jesus in my life. No one would hurt us. My confidence was in Jesus not me.

We sat opposite the two men. They didn't even look at us as we sat down. I said, "Hello," but there was nothing. It was like they were both blind and deaf. They didn't shift in their chairs. They didn't look in our direction. They just sat enjoying their individual quiet time, no smiles, no chatting to each other; it was just quiet. The waiter arrived with drinks for my husband and me. I took a sip of my drink and smiled at the two men wearing sunglasses. "Hello," I said again but still nothing. "Do you want to know something amazing?" I asked them, but neither of them spoke or turned their heads to look at me. They just continued to ignore me. In my mind I said, "Jesus, I know you've got me. I want to talk about you to others. I know you're in control. My confidence is in you." I felt my husband tap my knee; it was a sign to stop but I couldn't. I just loved God so much, I wanted everyone to know about Jesus in my life. Happily, I said, "I was baptised a week ago, God is real, it's the best decision of my life." I'd said it, I had to get it out, I had to tell someone about it. I couldn't understand why, but I needed everyone who didn't know that God was real.

At that moment the first gentleman took his glasses off, looked at me and said, "I believe in God. God saved me when I was in Germany. Hello sister."

Then the gentleman sitting next to him said, "I'm a Catholic, and I know about God too." My husband was shocked as the two ruthless looking characters smoking cigars at the back of the ship now took their sunglasses off and each told us about their lives. The Catholic man sang in a choir. His choir had even performed at the Vatican. The other gentleman told me about his wonderful wife and two daughters and how God had saved him decades earlier. It was unexpected the time we shared as these two men smoked their cigars. They each shook my husband's hand, and we continued to wave to each other over the next few weeks of our cruise whenever we saw each other.

It made me think about how, we never know what others have been through. We don't know at a glance the hardship someone once had but God knows all because He sees all, He hears all, and He loves us all. We don't need to judge a book by its cover; we only need to love others the same way Jesus loves us.

Crazy Cat And Bird Friend

I have a friend; she's more like a sister to me. I've known her for decades, and she is one of my best friends. When I was angry Ange, I use to say to her, that if in life we had to be friends with a crazy cat loving friend or a crazy bird loving friend she had ticked both boxes because she loved cats and always owned at least two cats. She also fed birds in her neighbourhood. The birds would all appear at her home every afternoon. She even hand fed small, injured birds. I thought she was crazy, but she just loved animals. She also had a dog; they were never small dogs, they were always dogs where their head as they stood beside you, reached the top of your thigh.

When my family and I visited her and her family whilst I was angry Ange, she would always feed the birds at a distance from us in the afternoons. They didn't own any birds of their own, but her husband built a bird aviary for their cats because they both knew I was scared of birds and cats. If one of her cats appeared near us, they would always put it in the bird aviary so it could sit with us, but it couldn't come near me. No other friends we had feared her cats, but it was something they did for me. I loved my friend, and she was important to me.

I had a fear of birds - I don't know how it started. I didn't recall ever being attacked by any bird; they were ok to look at from a distance, which meant it had to be more than 10 meters away from me. I remember many times at home; I had an external clothesline and it was a mobile one. I'd hang a load of washing on it on our back decking area and when the clothes were dry, I'd just fold my external clothesline up and put it away in our storage room until it was required again. The back decking area was like a laundry drying room for me because it was a large open space with no windows but had a roof.

If I was outside hanging washing and a bird arrived, I'd side eye the bird, and kept an eye on it, always checking my peripheral vision. It didn't matter how big or small the bird was. It was the fact that a bird was even close to me that would freak me out. If it was four meters from me, it was a side eye glance. If it came closer, I was wondering if it would attack me because we had a lot of swooping birds in our area. They would swoop down towards your head, but none ever did that to me; I was just scared of any and every bird.

Often, if I was hanging washing out and a bird appeared, I'd side eye it. If a second bird appeared I'd think to myself, "Oh, you brought a friend," and if a third bird appeared, it was too much. I'd always run into my house, lock the back sliding door and take photos, sending urgent text messages to my husband and children advising them I couldn't finish their laundry because I felt like I was under attack from three birds just watching me. If the birds walked around on my back deck, I'd take more photos thinking they were surveying the area, and I needed security for assistance. This happened for decades but when I found God and Jesus was in my life, the fear of cats and birds just stopped. I didn't do anything for it to stop; I didn't even worry about it, but one day, it just stopped.

I tried telling my husband how God had taken my fear of birds away but he remembered the decades of pictures I'd sent of not being able to hang out washing and photos where I'd circled birds on our back deck crying for security assistance. He'd smile then nod and say nothing. The photos requesting help from a bird on our back deck just stopped, the washing got hung out, and my husband and children never thought about it again.

My husband didn't believe me when I said Jesus took my fear of birds away. It was ok if he didn't believe me; I left it with the Lord. Not everyone would understand how something like a fear of birds for decades could just stop.

My husband and I sat outside one day eating lunch. He sat opposite me facing the open area of our back deck whilst I sat on the other side of our outdoor lounge, the chaise section, facing inside the house. I noticed my husband's eyes widen as he went to take a bite from his sandwich. Then a swooping bird landed next to me on the lounge. Before my husband could shoo the bird away, I turned and said to the bird standing next to me," Off you go. I'm having lunch." It looked at me then turned and walked off. It was too lazy to fly away and just walked to the end of the lounge I was sitting on, like it was on a pedestrian crossing. My husband had no words, but I reminded him that Jesus had taken my fear of birds away.

My crazy cat and bird loving friend called, and she wanted to know if I was free for a catch up, maybe go to the shops together then come back to her place for a coffee and cake. We would catch up together in two days. I hadn't seen my friend in a few months and was excited.

That night, when everyone else in my home was asleep. I went to my old office that I now used as a prayer room. I closed the door and prayed for my unbelieving friend.

> "Dear Lord, it's me. I'm catching up with my friend in two days; can you please give me scripture to share with her, so she knows you are real."

But I heard nothing. The next morning, I thought about how I only had one more day before I would see my friend and I prayed again the same prayer as the day before.

> "Dear Lord, it's me. I'm catching up with my friend in one day; can you please give me scripture to share with her, so she knows you are real."

But still nothing. That night and the morning of our catch up, I went back into my prayer room and asked for scripture but still heard nothing.

I got into my car and prayed in my mind as I drove. I reminded the Lord I was driving to my friend's place and asked if He had any scripture for me to share with her, but it was still silent. I turned my Christian worship music on. I thought to myself, that it's going to be a good day. As I neared my friend's home at a set of lights, I prayed again in my mind, reminding the Lord I was only five minutes from my friend's home. "Any scripture?" I asked, but it was still silent. As I parked my car outside my friend's home, I prayed again,

> "Dear Lord, it's me. I'm at my friend's home. Maybe I had my Christian worship music on too loud as I drove and I couldn't hear you. Can you please give me some scripture so I can talk about you to my unbelieving friend, so she knows you are real," but it was silent. A thought from scripture came to mind about not worrying.

I thanked the Lord for my friend and the day He had prepared for us and went in to see my friend.

She drove us to the shops, and as she drove, I started praying in my mind again to ask the Lord for scripture, but it was still silent. The Lord had a plan for today I thought, I trusted Jesus. My friend and I talked while she drove to the shop we planned to go to. It was a large warehouse, had lots of bargains, and it didn't take much time to fill the trolley.

When we got back to my friend's place, I hadn't prayed again because I realized that the Lord was in control. He had prepared the day for us to just spend time together and I was grateful. As we made coffee and walked outside to her outdoor setting, one of my friend's cats appeared; it was white, and its fur was really long. It walked up towards me, and I stood still watching it walk majestically. It rubbed its face and body across the bottom part of my legs as I watched it walk. It was our first interaction in over 10 years. My friend looked at me and then at her cat and asked, "Are you ok?" I nodded and told her how Jesus had taken my fear of cats away. She looked back at her white cat, it never came near people, it only went near family members who lived in her home, yet it had made an appearance today. She reasoned out loud that maybe her cat could tell I was no longer scared of it and that's why it came out to see me and walk so closely to me.

We had our coffee and I stood in the middle of my friend's backyard as she cut up cake slices for us to share. It was lovely standing in the sunshine. My friend had a table and bench chairs in the middle of her yard. She had other seating underneath a roofed area of her backyard, but I was enjoying the sunshine. As I stood still, her dog came up to me on my right, I patted her dog on its head and greeted it. My friend came out with a plate of cut up cake for us to share as her second cat, that looked like a tiger with stripes, came towards me. It jumped up on the bench seat beside me on my left as I patted it. I looked to my right and saw my friend just standing still watching for the first time as I interacted with her striped cat. Then a swooping bird dived down from her fence toward me. I stood still, knowing Jesus was in control and I had nothing to fear. It swooped, not towards my head but to my feet. I looked down at the swooping bird and acknowledged it. My friend was speechless as she stood frozen and looking at me as I stood in the middle of her backyard next to her bench seating. Her dog was on my right with his head pressed against my leg, her cat was on my left as I patted it and a swooping bird stood at my feet. The cat, the bird and the dog were within 30 centimeters of each other yet none of the three animals were attacking each other; they just stood next to me. No words were spoken between my friend and me about what happened. Maybe she thought her eyes were playing tricks on her. I didn't need to say anything because God was making Himself known to my unbelieving friend without me quoting any scripture.

When I left my friend's place, I drove and prayed in my mind as Christian music played softly in the car to thank the Lord for the day He had prepared for us.

The Lord reminded me that when He is silent, it doesn't mean He hasn't heard me, it just means He is preparing something for me. Always for our good and His glory. The Lord reminded me that though I loved my friend, He loved her first.

These Doctors Are Crazy

I have another best friend; we met at work years earlier. She's married and has children and our kids grew up together and they continue to be friends even as young adults.

She had this amazing skill of being able to look at her children in a particular way when we were all gathered together. They just knew from a glance their Mum needed a glass of water, a hug or even an item of food from the other end of the table. I didn't know how she did it. I tried the glance at my own children when they were young, but they just thought I was being weird.

We'd been friends for decades. We shared everything in life together, our ups and our downs. There was no filter, it was an honest relationship, and I loved her and she loved me too. Whenever I saw her, I'd always give her a hug. I wasn't a hugger as angry Ange, but she was someone who I had chosen as family.

She came from a loving family. Her father had passed years before I met her, but I knew her mum. My friend and her mum were extremely close, almost like best friends. It was a sad day when her Mum passed. I didn't go to the funeral, but I knew what it was like to lose someone who you loved. She loved her Mum like I'd loved my Grandpa.

Not long after her Mum passed my friend told us how she had been diagnosed with a blood cancer. She was now immuno-compromised. The doctors had found treatment for her. Her blood cancer meant that her platelet count would drop randomly. If it dropped too low then it meant her blood thinned out and if she even got a paper cut at those times, she could bleed to death. The treatment kept her platelet count at a normal level, so her blood wasn't too thin. When I was angry Ange, I wondered why such a wonderful person would get such an illness. Why did bad things like cancer happen to good people? I'd think to myself that maybe if God was real, it meant He didn't like us and was punishing us.

My best friends and I started a group chat together, it was called 'besties'. I'm not sure who started it or even how it started, I just remember us all having this one messaging group that we could message updates to each other or send photos to each other about our days. It was always random messages to ask how the other person was going, wishing each other a lovely weekend, and asking when we would have our next catch up. We also used the group chat for guidance if things went wrong or we needed each other's advice on something that was happening in our homes. I loved our best friends chat group because there was never a filter. We all had a relationship of being as subtle as a head butt with each other, and no one was offended by another.

When I found God was real, I tried talking to my friend about it, but she told me she didn't believe in God. She believed there would be a heaven but not God because she'd tried praying to God when her Mum became unwell but her Mum still died. So, if God was loving, then how could he allow that to happen? It was the first time in 20 years that one person was offended by another, so I stopped talking about God to her.

Months went past and I received a message in our group chat from my friend. The treatment her doctors and specialists had put her on was no longer working. She was having regular blood tests to confirm her chemo treatment was working and it had been working properly for over 10 years but now the three specialists she had, all reached out to her. They had each received individual results from her latest blood test and they told her that her blood results were not good. The treatment she was on was no longer working. There was no alternative treatment. If her platelet count continued to drop, she would die.

I tried calling my friend, but she didn't pick up. She was too upset to talk. I didn't know what to do so I reached out to all the women at my home church, as we had a sisterhood chat group together. We often used the chat group to give encouragement to one another. It was our way of staying connected to each other during the week before we gathered together the following Sunday with our families at our home church.

I told them about my friend and asked them all to pray for my unbelieving friend. I told them about the blood results and how I didn't want my friend to die. That day and for the next few days, we all prayed for my friend and asked Jesus to heal her.

Two more days passed, and I decided to try calling my friend since I'd received no further updates from her in our best friends' group chat. Our group chat had gone silent in the last few days. She didn't pick up the call, and I thought to myself that she must still be upset so I messaged our besties chat group.

ME – I haven't heard from you. I've tried calling you, but I'm worried about you. How are you going?

FRIEND – I'm good. These doctors are all crazy. One minute, I have three separate specialists telling me my treatment is no longer working because my blood results were not good but a few days later, they've each contacted me to say all my blood results are good now. They've said I can continue with the same treatment. How did they get it so wrong and make me worry? They must be crazy.

I fell to my knees and cried.

"Thank-you Lord for saving my friend."

CHAPTER 7

FOOTSTEPS OF JESUS IN MY LIFE AS ANGRY ANGE

Introduction Revisited - God During Those Times

Hindsight is an amazing thing. So often we look back at our lives and tell stories of our hurt, of our pain, of how someone either did something to us that they shouldn't have done or treated us a way that was not right. Sometimes we tell stories of good times but its more the stories of hurt that shape us to who we choose to become. Not many of us will look back to look for evidence of where God was during those times. When we look back to search for God through those painful times, it gives us a better understanding of gratitude.

If I think back to my terrible childhood and youth, I now see how God was watching over me and protecting me the whole time. He had a plan for my life, but I just couldn't understand it till now.

When I was first abused at eight my stepfather started by making me sit on his bed that he shared with my mother and forced me take all my clothes off while he stood over me with his belt. After he belted me and I had welts on my body or blood from how hard the belt had hit my skin, he made me lay down so he could sexually abuse me. I remembered screaming for help. I remembered my mother was home, I screamed for her to save me but she didn't come. I screamed that I was dying and that I felt like he was killing me, but she still didn't come into the room. I remembered walking out after he had finished sexually abusing me, then he told me to get out and clean my body because I was filthy. As I walked out of his bedroom, I saw the television was on but with no sound, it had been muted. I looked and saw my birth mother smiling at me. She had heard me screaming but smiled and gestured for me to go have a shower, like everything was ok. Her smile said it all - I deserved it. In the bathroom I sat on the cold tiles crying silently and, in my mind, asking God if I ever survived this house of torture, if I ever lived to be an adult, if one day I could have my own family who could love me and He answered that prayer. I have a wonderful husband and amazing children.

My stepfather who stood over me from eight years of age, was someone who had given in to his sinful desires. No one should have their childhood innocence taken from them, but he did that to me and felt no shame for his actions. After I moved away at 19, I was fearful of ever running into him again. It wasn't until much later in life, when I had a husband and children of my own, that I found out what had happened to my stepfather. Many years earlier after I left that house of torture, he became extremely unwell. The doctors said the only way he could survive was to have his legs amputated. He was wheelchair bound for the rest of his life, unable to stand over anyone again. The Lord had punished him for what he did to me. I just never knew until after I found God.

My birth mother survived by telling lies to others. She told the pastor at her Seventh Day Adventist church that she was so rich she would pay for the pastor's child to go to university. When the time came for her to pay, a few years later she fled that church because she had no money. It was her way during those years for others to look up to her and tell her she was a good person. She had stolen inheritances that were not meant for her. She had received the superannuation my stepfather earnt when she hadn't worked a day in her life. She had stolen money from others and been so convincing with her lies that they themselves became homeless still thinking my birth mother would pay them back but because of her gambling, it was all gone.

I bumped into an old friend of my mother's one day after I'd escaped their house of torture. My mother's friend was rummaging through the garbage tin for food. I called out to her, and she looked up at me. I went and asked her if she needed some help, if she needed some food but she screamed at me to get away from her. I rang the police to report my mother's crimes. I tried to do it anonymously until they asked why I was reporting her and I told them my birth mother was scamming others for funds that did not belong to her to pay for her gambling addiction. I never heard back from them.

My mother lived a meaningless life trying to work out her next lie until she died of cancer about three years ago. Even when I found out she'd died, I contemplated going to her funeral to throw acid on her face just to make sure she wasn't lying and the funeral wasn't a lie. I needed proof that this wasn't another way of her making money by scamming others or trying to lie to me.

I'd picked up my bible for the first time in years, trying to make sense of how I was feeling. This was because three years ago, I knew about God, but it was more like a business transaction where I'd pull God out like a business card when I needed Him, hoping He would hear me. I sought the God my Grandpa had talked about, the one my Grandpa said loved everyone and had no favorites. All I got from reading different passages in the bible was to walk with love and kindness. So I told family who rang me - my aunts, my uncles and cousins that the bible says to walk with love and kindness. I told each of them to go to my birth mother's funeral if they wanted. I told them all, that there had to be a kind or loving moment they'd exchanged with my birth mother themselves throughout the decades when she was alive, but most couldn't think of anything! In the end, at my birth mother's funeral, out of more than 100 immediate family members only six turned up to the funeral, two of whom were my brother and his partner.

It took some time to forgive her for all the things she'd done to me, but the Lord showed me that holding onto the offenses and not forgiving her was like serving myself a glass of poison. Drinking the poison and then waiting for my birth mother to be affected by the poison I'd drunk. I forgave her and left it with the Lord who will judge her. I realized no large amount of sin is worse than one small white lie because all are a sin to God. I forgave her and the Lord took all the pain, hurt, and anxiety that I used to feel about her away.

I was angry with my aunts and uncles for a long time. This was years before I knew God was real. One of my older aunts rang me to wish me a happy birthday. I told her to delete my number because she had crossed the line. She was the same aunt who my Grandpa lived with; she was the same aunt who stopped me going to my Grandpa's funeral. She was dead to me.

Decades later, this aunt was diagnosed with cancer. Treatment wasn't an option because she'd left it too late to have checks done and by the time the cancer had been discovered, she was terminal and didn't have much time left. Before that aunt's death, she rang me from her death bed, she apologized for everything she'd done to me and asked for my forgiveness. I thought about how I'd also hurt others and was willing to forgive her. However, before I could say, "Yes, I forgive you," she told me she had my Grandma's jewellery and was leaving it to me after she died. I asked her to give it to me now and she said I had to wait until after she died but she needed my forgiveness first, so I forgave her.

After she died, I didn't go to her funeral but I went to collect my Grandma's jewellery from my dead aunt's husband. She'd lied. The contents of the large jewellery box were full of scrap costume jewellery. I checked with other aunts and uncles, and they confirmed none of it belonged to their Mum. I was happy for any piece of jewellery. It didn't matter if it was costume jewellery or not. If it belonged to my Grandma, I wanted it, but it was all a lie. None of it belonged to my Grandma. I took all the jewellery still in the large jewellery box to the local shopping centre and dumped it in the large garbage bin out the back of the shopping centre. Later that week I prayed about this dead aunt. "God if you're real, I don't forgive her anymore, please send that aunt to hell."

I've since spent time with the Lord about this specific aunt. I've also spent time reviewing scripture. I found that the bible says to love others. It says the Lord forgives us as easily as we forgive others. The bible also says that it is each individual's responsibility to decide for themselves on whether to love God or deny God. If they love God and believe in Jesus and what Jesus did on the cross as the son of God for their past, present and future sins, then heaven is their eternal destination. If they deny God, then they have chosen after their death to be far from God's love and kindness for eternity in hell. My prayers to send my aunt to hell, were not biblical. The same would be said for praying to send a non-believer to heaven after they died; it's not biblical. We don't have a way to pray anyone to either heaven or hell after they've taken their last breath because they make that choice before their last breath. We are only human. We don't make suggestions on our preferences of other's eternal destinations to God because only God knows all hearts.

Regarding the family I lost, some of them came back, some didn't because the damage had been done. My words and actions at the time had cut too deeply. Some of the others who hadn't left, I held resentment to. I couldn't understand why they never helped me when I was young but were readily available now that I was an adult and I didn't need them anymore. I've spent a lot of time after finding God trying to love them, trying to help them. I sometimes still held offenses and other times I just wanted them to be saved. I found sometimes it's easier to be kind and love a stranger than those who said they loved me but hurt me because strangers hadn't done anything wrong to me.

Through prayer and seeking the Lord's advice, I found my aunts and uncles are broken people living in a broken world. No one is perfect but Jesus was perfect for everyone and showed us how to walk with love and kindness regardless of how others treated us. Jesus had family and friends reject Him too, so He understood what I was going through. I've stopped arguing with my aunts and uncles. I sometimes remember back to when I was little and how they were all like my big brothers and sisters. I've forgiven all of them and I love each of them deeply. None of us can do anything about the past but if we focus too much on the past then we miss the gifts of today, the present. Without the Lord that wouldn't have happened.

Since finding the Lord, I've rebuilt some relationships I used to have with friends or other family. The ones that haven't been rebuilt, I now understand the pain that I've caused them was too hurtful. Either way, I still pray for them because it's what scripture asks us to do.

When I first became a Christian, I wanted everyone to know God was real. I contemplated watching for the alerts on my security camera and running out to people walking their dogs past my home to give them the good news. My pastor suggested against it, so I didn't.

I still enjoy talking about my love of God to everyone because, as my pastor's wife says, "God can't steer a parked car, and you can't kill a spiritually dead person." She is always so encouraging for me. Much like my church community, my spiritual family of brothers and sisters have helped me walk this narrow path but I've now learnt to watch for the footsteps of Jesus in other people's lives. If God is working on them and asks me to be quiet, I don't need to say anything, but if they talk about God or ask about my testimony, I'm ready and willing.

Looking for the footsteps of Jesus in anyone's life is important, because without it, it would be like spending hours talking to a wall. It's exhausting, it's meaningless but with God everything is wonderful, everything has meaning and we each have a purpose. I don't need to worry about everyone, but I just need to understand - the people I love, God loved them first.

Forgiveness was an important part of this new journey I'm on; it helped heal my own brokenness.

> Matthew 6:14-15 NIV [14] "For if you forgive other people when they sin against you, your heavenly Father will also forgive you. [15] But if you do not forgive others their sins, your Father will not forgive your sins."

Forgiveness also meant letting go of things I didn't need to be holding onto. When I forgave those who hurt me in my past, the Lord removed all the emotions I had towards them away from me. I can now talk about everything from my childhood as though it's about someone else. I'm no longer triggered by the past. Forgiveness played a big part in that growth and Jesus healed me of the hurt and pain.

The verse from scripture that use to worry me was,

> Matthew 22:14 NKJV [14] "For many are called, but few are chosen."

I remembered hearing that verse one time as a child. No one ever explained the meaning of it to me, but I used to think that verse meant God preselected those who he wanted to go to heaven. I often thought about it as God rejecting me, but it doesn't mean that at all. It's a very encouraging verse but I had to drop my pride, humble myself and ask the Lord for guidance to better understand the verse. When you think about Jesus' character of love for others, He didn't go to the cross and die for a few selected individuals. He went to the cross for everyone, their past, present and future sins then offered it to us as a free gift for our salvation, not through anything we did but because of everything He did for all of us. He just asked us to believe because:

> For many are called = God calls everyone
> But few are chosen = but few choose God

It puts a whole new meaning to that verse when we realize it's God trying to talk to us to turn to Him instead of us feeling rejected.

Here's my prayer for you:

> "Dear God,
>
> I pray for the person reading this message. I pray they understand how through our weakness you are always strong for us. I pray that they understand when we fail, you never fail. When we do something wrong, you remind us

that we don't need to be perfect. I pray they forgive others who have misspoken or treated them wrong because then their own healing journeys can begin. Lord, please search their heart. Remind them of your love for them so they can seek you themselves to find your truth. Please bring people into their lives like you did with mine, to encourage them to make the first move, to turn to you or to walk closer with you. We never have to worry because you are always in control. We never have to doubt whether you love us because you sent your only son to die on a cross for our sins. Thank you, Lord,

In Jesus name, Amen."

Pride Came In Unannounced - God During Those Times

Definition of Pride according to the Oxford dictionary:

> 'Pride - (Noun) a feeling of deep pleasure or satisfaction derived from one's own achievements, the achievements of those with whom one is closely associated, or from qualities or possessions that are widely admired'.

God created a perfect world but we all kind of stuffed it up.

So many want riches but what for? Is it to feed the hungry or their own pride?

So many want to be better than others but what for? Is it to set a good example or to have opportunities to look down on others?

So many want to pretend that everything is okay and their lives are amazing, but what for? Is it so others won't worry about you, or is it so others can envy you and you can get more likes on social media?

Being prideful and doing everything my way seemed ok as Angry Ange but when I read the bible and realized that one of the most beautiful angels (Satan) had become a demon because of pride then I wondered, what would happen to us humans if we failed to humble ourselves and be grateful to God.

I was a very prideful person, but pride is something that sneaks up on you, it doesn't reveal itself and say that I am here. Pride doesn't come with a warning like food labels; it always comes in unannounced.

I lived my life sometimes as a very shallow person. Thinking how, in every situation, it was about me, but the bible taught me the importance of others. The bible taught me to lift others up, love others, and forgive others. The bible taught me that when we have God in our lives, we must walk with the light of Christ for others so they can notice their need for God in their own lives.

Each of the examples of me being prideful serves to highlight how God was able to use each of these examples to directly show me how not to behave. These lessons have taught me how not to treat others. Jesus reminded me in scripture to love others like how he loves us. If pride is in the way, it's hard to be grateful to God when it's only about ourselves and our achievements. No one can earn salvation; it's a free gift from God but we must humble ourselves and be honest because God sees all hearts.

When God comes into our lives and teaches each of us about pride he knows we will never be perfect but how wonderful it is when walking with the Lord that we now have eyes to see when pride makes an appearance; it doesn't stay unnoticed anymore.

> Proverbs 16:18 NKJV [18] "Pride goes before destruction,
> And a haughty spirit before a fall."

Taking Control – I'm In Charge - God During Those Times

Being in control was all I needed when I was Angry Ange. I dictated the direction of all my steps. I made the best choices for me. Putting my trust only in me.

I was so foolish to think I could control every narrative, and every situation because I was only headed in the wrong direction.

Life got harder the more I tried to take control. It's burdensome and made me weary. It made me anxious, stressed and angry all the time. I read in Matthew 11 that when Jesus is in control, l didn't need to be the strongest person in the room.

> Matthew 11:28-30 NLT [28] "Then Jesus said, 'Come to me, all of you who are weary and carry heavy burdens, and I will give you rest. [29] Take my yoke upon you. Let me teach you, because I am humble and gentle at heart, and you will find rest for your souls. [30] For my yoke is easy to bear, and the burden I give you is light.'"

The bible taught me that God is always in control, even when I've lost control. God sees everything we do, everything we say, every thought we've ever had, and still says to come to Him. Nothing is a burden for the Lord. Jesus taking control of my life was the best decision I've ever made. I sometimes even now get things wrong, but because Jesus leads me, I'm grateful for his guidance and gentle corrections. I'm no longer on the highway to hell.

The way I thought I controlled everything for decades, the trouble that I could have got into, the trouble that I could have caused for others, the unnecessary pain I could have caused myself if God wasn't taking care of me. I look back and notice it more now.

Looking back at the drive to see my Grandpa, to say goodbye to him, only now do I see the footsteps of Jesus from that time. Driving at more than double the speed limit, I'd driven 20 minutes instead of 40 minutes to my older aunt's house that day. Driving like a crazy person trying to kill myself on the road and screaming to the God my Grandpa believed in because I felt like I had nothing left to live for. Every intersection was a green light; no one else was on the road at such a busy time in the afternoon. God had been taking care of me that afternoon, even when I didn't know if He really existed or not, even when I didn't think I was worthy. When I'm faithless, God is faithful. When I fail, God never fails.

Thinking back to my wedding, God was helping me heal my brokenness and grieving heart when I didn't think God was real. He had found a wonderful man for me to be my husband, and He had organized for my uncle to fly to our wedding. The timing was perfect.

When I was first saved and experienced the new birth of God's Holy Spirit coming into my life, the thoughts about my pending death came to mind one night. I tried smoking as many cigarettes as I could to stop the thoughts and emotions coming to mind but it still came up. I tried reading the bible to get rid of the thoughts but that didn't work either, so I prayed and asked God to help me understand what was happening. I believed in God now; Angry Ange was dead but why was this memory surfacing? Because it was dug so deep and I tried to never think about it since it made me sad thinking about the days until I would die.

I asked God for help, pleading for his Holy Spirit to show me the truth and the memory of the fortune teller instantly came to mind in particular the ending where the fortune teller told me he could read my mind. God had brought up a painful memory and showed me that I didn't need to fear because the fortune teller was a demon in disguise and only God could read my mind. I was grateful that I now understood that truth because for years I thought the enemy could read my mind and that was the reason I had always said half-truths in my prayers whenever I prayed, hoping God would hear me. The truth is only God is omnipotent (all-powerful), omnipresent (everywhere at once), and omniscient (all-knowing).

"Why God?" I used to say, but now I realize that when I was Angry Ange, I was strong for me, I knew what was best for me, and I thought I understood what life was all about. If I was unsure about anything I'd make another appointment with a fortune teller because they said they could tell me my future and talk to my dead relatives. They did it by telling me things I hadn't shared with anyone or through their special cards or holding an item of jewellery that I always wore and didn't take off, like my wedding ring. It gave me comfort knowing my relatives were ok and they could still guide me to make better choices but reading the bible and finding out that our families and friends who had died can no longer communicate with us made me think about where these fortune tellers were getting their information from. Then I read in the bible that only God knows the future.

I wondered if only God could tell the future, and how these fortune tellers could tell me anything about my future. Through prayer, Jesus showed me what Satan had used to create fear about death for three decades but God had instead used for my good and His glory. The enemy told me I would die at 54, that's my current age, but I no longer fear that memory. I no longer spend any time in the day thinking about my funeral; I no longer worry about it because God has a plan for me. Watching for where God has been throughout my life and where He is in my life now creates feelings of love, hope, and joy, not sadness, anger, grief and worry.

I also wondered how all these fortune tellers could tell me anything about my past or why I often used to think that maybe one of my children or family members was a reincarnation of an old relative who had died.

I read in the bible that there were such things as lying spirits. I read that they were the teachings of demons.

I also read in the bible that God specifically tells us not to seek these fortune tellers.

> Deuteronomy 18:10-12 AMP [10] "There shall not be found among you anyone who makes his son or daughter pass through the fire [as a sacrifice], one who uses divination and fortune-telling, one who practices witchcraft, or one who interprets omens, or a sorcerer, [11] or one who casts a charm or spell, or a medium, or a spiritist, or a necromancer [who seeks the dead]. [12] For everyone who does these things is utterly repulsive to the Lord."

Fortune tellers have been around since one third of the angels in heaven were cast down to earth because of Satan. Satan the devil, convinced these other heavenly angels to try and overthrow God because Satan hated that God loved us humans so much. Satan also hated that how regardless of how many times we failed that God still loved us. Satan, who was full of pride, wanted to become like God to be worshipped himself.

The apostle Paul even wrote about his interaction with a fortune teller in Acts of the Apostles in the bible.

Acts 16:16- 18 NLT [16] "One day as we were going down to the place of prayer, we met a slave girl who had a spirit that enabled her to tell the future. She earned a lot of money for her masters by telling fortunes. [17] She followed Paul and the rest of us, shouting, 'These men are servants of the Most High God, and they have come to tell you how to be saved.' [18] This went on day after day until Paul got so exasperated that he turned and said to the demon with her, "I command you in the name of Jesus Christ to come out of her." And instantly it left her.

Because of these findings in the bible, I stopped seeking any mediums, fortune tellers, psychics or clairvoyants.

Regarding reincarnation, no one is reincarnated. The bible explains that we die once not multiple times.

> Hebrews 9:27 NIV [27] "Just as people are destined to die once, and after that to face judgment."

Now that I have Jesus in my life, I seek the Lord's guidance for my future plans. If anyone has news to share with me that they claim is from God, I'll test it exactly like it says in scripture. I do that by praying about it or checking if the news they've given me contradicts scripture or not. God doesn't lie and if someone tells me something that doesn't match the bible, then the message is not from God.

> 1 John 4:1 NLT [1] "Dear friends, do not believe everyone who claims to speak by the Spirit. You must test them to see if the spirit they have comes from God. For there are many false prophets in the world."

If, like me, you've spent time with fortune tellers or wondered about reincarnation or practised any form of witchcraft (like my birth mother did) don't over analyze until you paralyze in your thoughts about it. It's simple, just stop and seek God as Jesus reminds us with scripture in the bible.

Matthew 7:8 NIV [8] "For everyone who asks receives; the one who seeks finds; and to the one who knocks, the door will be opened."

Coveting What Wasn't Mine - God During Those Times

Riches and treasures for this life was what it was all about for me back then as Angry Ange. Looking at what others had and what I felt I was missing out on were my main focus.

If someone had a better house than me, I wanted something grander. If someone had a better life than me, I wanted to surpass them with riches of my own.

Reading the bible, especially the New Testament, has helped me to understand the importance of what is temporal verses what is eternal.

A house is just a house, it doesn't matter the size but what makes it a home are those who live within its walls. A house will always require some form of maintenance and one day the homes we hold so dear will one day all be turned to dust. Others will eventually change it or demolish it, so what we hold as valuable is only temporary.

Eternal matters of importance are the treasures of our own hearts. The treasures that are not easily destroyed.

> Matthew 6:19-21 NLT [19] "Don't store up treasures here on earth, where moths eat them and rust destroys them, and where thieves break in and steal. [20] Store your treasures in heaven, where moths and rust cannot destroy, and thieves do not break in and steal. [21] Wherever your treasure is, there the desires of your heart will also be."

Treasures of my heart are no longer temporary. They include my family and friends being saved so they can choose Jesus also and go to heaven - the thought of bringing a lost soul to the Lord. They are the new riches and treasures that I want. Money plays no significance because you cannot buy your way into heaven. If everything belongs to God then that would mean our money does too, but if you can't buy yourself into heaven, what use is it to hold onto for our own selfish desires, for temporal treasures?

I also think back now that I have Jesus in my life to see his footsteps even back then. I remember being so angry at the time about not winning Secret Sound and missing out on a deposit for a house for my family. However, now I realize decades later that if we had won that radio competition, when other family members moved from interstate, we would have lived over an hour away from them. Our children would not have grown up together and had the wonderful relationships they had as young cousins and now as young adults. We did buy a house; it was a lot smaller than the brand-new homes, but it was ours and our family lived 10 minutes away.

Losing Control - God During Those Times

Praying for someone who was sick and asking God to make them well again and praying for someone who was on their death bed and asking God to cure them. Praying for people and our prayers not being answered felt like a kick in the guts. Why did they not get better? Why did they still die? It was something that caused me to distance myself from God thinking I wasn't worthy or God wasn't real. In reality, I was angry with God because these were all people who were dear to my heart. I loved them and wanted them to be well, but I forgot that God loved them first.

If one person, who we love who knows God and has the Lord in their lives, when they die, they are in heaven with Jesus.

> John 14:3 NKJV [3] "And if I go and prepare a place for you, I will come again and receive you to Myself; that where I am, there you may be also."

I used to be angry about unanswered prayers and losing a loved one but the bible tells us that a day is like a thousand years to the Lord.

> 2 Peter 3:8 AMP [8] "Nevertheless, do not let this one fact escape your notice, beloved, that with the Lord one day is like a thousand years, and a thousand years is like one day."

God sees more than what we see in 24 hours. He sees the bigger picture. If someone we loved dies, it doesn't mean God is being mean, or we are unworthy; it just means He can see through one person's death that many in their families can be saved. It's not about us being worthy or unworthy, it's about God loving everyone and wanting everyone to be saved.

> John 3:16 NKJV [16] "For God so loved the world that he gave His only begotten Son, that whoever believes in Him should not perish but have everlasting life."

That white light that I was ashamed about before I knew the Lord was actually Satan trying to steer me away from God. I never knew until I read the bible that the enemy could disguise himself as a white light.

> 2 Corinthians 11:14 NIV [14] "And no wonder, for Satan himself masquerades as an angel of light."

I've learnt that God's character is only love and encouragement.

> 1 John 4:7-8 NLT [7] "Dear friends, let us continue to love one another, for love comes from God. Anyone who loves is a child of God and knows God. [8] But anyone who does not love does not know God, for God is love."

The enemy's character is only deceit, lies and discouragement.

> John 8:44 NLT [44] ..."The devil...he was a murderer from the beginning. He has always hated the truth, because there is no truth in him. When he lies, it is consistent with his character; for he is a liar and the father of lies."

God doesn't make mistakes. He is perfect and when He forgives and says He will never remember our sins, He will blot them out forever, then that is the truth to believe instead of the lies.

> Isaiah 43:25 NLT [25] "I—yes, I alone—will blot out your sins for my own sake and will never think of them again."

God doesn't ask us to always be in control, but He does ask us to make a choice. God asks you to notice that you are a sinner and your need for God in your own life. God asks you to choose Him; it's your free will whether you do or you don't. God doesn't force Himself into your life, instead He makes Himself known to you and waits for you to invite Him into your life because it's the free will He gives you.

> James 4:7-8 NLT [7] "So humble yourselves before God. Resist the devil, and he will flee from you. [8] Come close to God, and God will come close to you. Wash your hands, you sinners; purify your hearts, for your loyalty is divided between God and the world."

To summarise, God answers all prayers. It may not be done the way we expect it but when we choose God, we realize just how much He actually loves us.

> Isaiah 55:8-9 NLT [8] "My thoughts are nothing like your thoughts," says the Lord. "And my ways are far beyond anything you could imagine. [9] For just as the heavens are higher than the earth, so my ways are higher than your ways and my thoughts higher than your thoughts."

Many blame God for everything that's wrong in the world, not knowing the bible tells us that Satan is the one who currently rules this world and helps us choose our sinful desires because of our sinful nature.

> John 12:31 NLT [31] "The time for judging this world has come, when Satan, the ruler of this world, will be cast out."

That's why we have such things as suicide, cancer, anxiety, etc. These things aren't from God but everyone blames God whether they believe in God or not because it's easier to blame God than find the truth for ourselves in the bible.

> Romans 8:28 NLT [28] "And we know that God causes everything to work together for the good of those who love God and are called according to his purpose for them."

When the bible says, "For the good of those who love God and are called according to his purpose for them," this means choosing God and His will for your life instead of trusting yourself. The bible tells us the first thing God will do for us when Jesus returns from the clouds is to wipe every tear from our eyes. Why would He do that? He does it out of love for everyone who chose God. Imagine choosing God and having Jesus in your life yet those you loved thought it was all nonsense. I can't begin to imagine the grief of having someone we love not going to heaven because they denied God, but God already knows most won't choose Him. He continues to reveal Himself to them, but they still deny Him because they are too clever to believe in something they cannot see, regardless of what their own heart tells them.

> Revelation 21:4 NLT [4] "He will wipe every tear from their eyes, and there will be no more death or sorrow or crying or pain. All these things are gone forever."

CHAPTER 8

SOME FAVOURITE BIBLE VERSES AND WHY

1. John 6:35 KJV [35] "And Jesus said unto them, I am the bread of life: he that cometh to me shall never hunger; and he that believeth on me shall never thirst."

John 6 verse 35 - was the first verse that really hit me when I read it. It was the first verse I memorized. I'm an islander and maybe at the start it was because this verse talked about food. It wasn't till later that I realized it meant so much more than just food for our stomachs. Jesus is the bread of life – He is the nourishment for our souls - the word of God that never lies and never fails us. Having a meal with the Lord involved sitting down and reading the bible, asking the Lord for His Holy Spirit to teach me. Believing in someone you cannot see but knowing in your heart, mind and soul that without Him there is no growth, no understanding because Jesus is the giver of living waters that makes us never thirst again. Life without Jesus was meaningless.

2. Romans 1:12 NLT [12] "When we get together, I want to encourage you in your faith, but I also want to be encouraged by yours."

Romans 1 verse 12 - Encouragement is about the importance of others; it wasn't something I used to do before God came into my life. As Angry Ange, I thought encouragement was spending my precious time explaining how to do a job for ME because everything revolved around ME. It wasn't until Jesus showed me about encouragement and the importance of OTHERS (not me) that I finally understood. When I was Angry Ange I never knew that anger is like a foothold for the devil. I did some terrible things to others but found no shame in my behavior until the Lord gave me eyes to see and I realized it's not all about me. It's about others also having Jesus to open their eyes to the truth, to open their ears to hear his whisper. For Jesus to lead them on their journey of the narrow path of righteousness for themselves. It's a meaningful life and because of Jesus I have purpose. I love encouragement. I can find encouragement in most things now only because of God in my life. I love hearing others talk about what's happening in their life and what the Lord is doing. I love talking about my love for God. It's a meaningful life and because of Jesus I have purpose.

3. Psalms 16:8 NLT [8] "I know the Lord is always with me. I will not be shaken, for he is right beside me."

Psalm 16 verse 8 is a verse I used to say when I was worried. It helped calm me because it was my reminder that the Lord is always with me. It reminded me that when I felt fearful, my confidence was in Jesus, not myself.

4. Psalms 23:1 NLT [1] "The Lord is my shepherd; I have all that I need."

The entirety of Psalm 23 is a favourite because it perfectly describes God's love for all of us who choose God. Jesus is the good shepherd. He reminds us that it's ok to rest, to walk with Him because it calms us and restores our souls as He leads us through a path of righteousness. I don't have to fear because Jesus will protect me. Our eternal home will be with the Lord.

5. Psalms 70:4 NKJV [4] "Let all those who seek You rejoice and be glad in You; And let those who love Your salvation say continually, 'Let God be magnified!'"

Psalm 70 verse 4 - I love this verse because it is my reminder of praise to Jesus for my salvation. The joy of knowing I was made right with God (all my sins forgiven) and go to heaven when this earthly body dies. I didn't earn it, it's a free gift from God, when we choose God. If I could thank God every moment of every day for what He's done in my life, the way He's changed me from the inside, it would never be enough. All the past hurt that I tried to escape for so long, has all gone. Different fears I had, the most fearful ones are gone. These are things I tried to run from or suppress for over 30 years - they're all gone. How do you say, "Thank you?" For me now, when words fail me, my heart constantly calls out to the Lord to say, "Thank you." The Lord asks us to be grateful for the free gift of salvation (life after death in heaven) that He offers us through everything Jesus has done for us.

Salvation means a lot of different things for different people. The people I know all think differently about what salvation is. Some don't read the bible, most belong to a religion and man-made rules, others distance themselves from God like I did for so long. Some believe there is no God, some believe in many Gods. Some believe two non-living atoms colliding in space created everything is a better choice for them than the thought that this world is perfectly designed by a Creator. Some think it's all about evolution, forgetting that Darwin didn't even know about DNA when he came up with his theory of evolution. Some think our earthly bodies get buried in the ground and wait till Judgment Day, and some think there is nothing. Some pray to God through Jesus earthly mother because they think she is now the queen of heaven and continue to hold onto certain practices seen as pagan even though it does not align with scripture. They feel their way through everything, including their own salvation. Some believe in reincarnation, some believe in crystals to keep themselves grounded, but forget we already have gravity.

We hear lots of stories from people who have had near death experiences. Most talk of a bright light, a black door, darkness, even heaven or hell but how many in comparison who have had a near death experience have said I saw nothing, that it's all meaningless? Salvation is knowing and trusting in God and what he offers as life after death. I've stopped reasoning with others because asking them a question about their soul is too much for some to think about. They are too clever for me; they are exactly who I used to be before Jesus came into my life and made it wonderful.

Scripture in the bible is clear on what Salvation is.

> Ephesians 2:8 AMP [8] For it is by grace [God's remarkable compassion and favor drawing you to Christ] that you have been saved [actually delivered from judgment and given eternal life] through faith. And this [salvation] is not of yourselves [not through your own effort], but it is the [undeserved, gracious] gift of God;

How hard is it to go to heaven?

Firstly, you MUST understand that you are a sinner. If you don't understand that you're a sinner then you are not being honest with yourself because if you've ever said one small white lie, it's a sin and is the same as having murdered someone, both are a sin. There is no such thing as a small sin or a big sin; they are all a sin and according to the bible the punishment for sin is death and hell for eternity. If you understand in your heart that you are a sinner, then understand you need a Saviour. Accept Jesus into your life because He gives you the gift of life after death willingly. You can't earn it, you cannot use money to pay for it, you cannot work for it with good deeds - you accept it through faith in Jesus.

> Romans 10:9-11 NIV [9] "If you declare with your mouth, 'Jesus is Lord,' and believe in your heart that God raised Him from the dead, you will be saved. [10] For it is with your heart that you believe and are justified, and it is with your mouth that you profess your faith and are saved. [11] As scripture says, 'Anyone who believes in Him will never be put to shame.'"

When the bible says that you are justified through Christ Jesus it is the same as saying, "just if I'd never sinned." Jesus took our hell punishment for all our (past, present and future) sins. It's what killed Jesus when He was nailed to the cross (our sins). God looked away from Jesus in that moment, and Jesus screamed out, "My God, my God why have you forsaken me?" because God cannot look upon sin. This was foretold thousands of years before Jesus was even born as a human about us needing a Saviour (Genesis 3) because none of us could live a perfect life and be sinless, yet Jesus did that for you, for me, for everyone, then offered it to us as a free gift.

All He asks is that we turn to Him, accept Jesus as our Savior and believe what He did on the cross for our past, present and future sins, the free gift from God. Let God be magnified.

Here's a fun fact: do you know what the chances are of anyone fulfilling a prophesy about the coming Messiah (our Savior) would be? If you imagine your home, regardless of how big or small it is, imagine for a moment that your home is full of normal sized golf balls. They don't flow out of your house when you open any doors; they only move about inside your home in every room. All of them are red and stacked and unboxed a meter high. Every room in your home just full of golf balls everywhere. As you walk through your home, the red golf balls move about because they are unboxed and a meter high. The chances of one prophesy being fulfilled is to walk into your home and to walk directly to the one golf ball underneath all the others and to pick the one white golf ball out from the rest, no detouring, no walking a different way to the one white golf ball but instead walking directly to it and picking it up. If anyone can do that one time it would seem like a miracle but Jesus fulfilled prophesy over 300 times before he was even nailed to the cross (another prophesy fulfilled) to die for us sinners (another prophecy fulfilled) to make us right with God (another prophecy fulfilled).

Some believe the Messiah (our Savior) hasn't come yet. Some will be led astray when the antichrist (Satan) comes as a man performing signs and wonders demanding all of us to worship him. Some will incorrectly worship the devil at that time because it's the only way to buy food. Others will put their trust in Jesus, knowing that this earthly life is temporary. Eternity is forever so whatever you decide then understand the decisions you make before your last breath determine where you get to spend eternity.

6. John 3:3 NIV [3] "Jesus replied, 'Very truly I tell you, no one can see the kingdom of God unless they are born again.'"

Regarding John 3, verse 3. I never knew about being born again (new birth) when I was part of any religious organization, maybe I wasn't listening. Most of the time I was thinking about other things when the person out the front of any church spoke. What does it mean to be born again? It basically means having God's Holy Spirit in you. No one can tell you if you've got it or not. Instead, Jesus shows you directly. Some people like me, experienced and felt something the day it happened, whereas others will think they've missed out because they didn't feel anything and push to the side the importance of what God is trying to show them. Through their own cleverness they overanalyze until they are paralysed in their own thoughts.

Here's my example: we've all heard of Billy Graham. If you haven't, then look him up. He was someone who loved God. He led millions of people to salvation, to understand God's truth, yet he never felt anything when he was reborn. Billy Graham intentionally sought God because he realized, he was a sinner. He prayed, "God, I don't know what's happening to me but as best as I know how, I give myself to you." Billy Graham made a decision, The bible is true, every word had been breathed out by God, and he just spoke about what the Lord had shown him and God did the rest. If you are unsure if you've experienced the new birth, pray about it. Ask Jesus for scripture. The confirmation of your salvation is directly between you and God.

7. John 1:17 NLT [17] "For the law was given through Moses, but God's unfailing love and faithfulness came through Jesus Christ."

This verse is my reminder; I'll never be perfect, but I don't have to be. Jesus shows us the love God has for us. Without Jesus, we cannot understand exactly what God has prepared for each of us. You will never be able to understand God's love for you without Jesus. If your thoughts conflict with scripture, then your thoughts are not from God. God loves us and He shows you His love through Jesus.

CHAPTER 9

WHAT HAVE I LEARNT IN LESS THAN TWO YEARS OF BEING A CHRISTIAN

During my short walk with Jesus in my life, I've found:

When I fail, God never fails.
When I'm faithless, God is faithful.
When I've lost control, God is in control.
When I feel like I've totally stuffed up and distance myself from God I've put a full stop on my journey, but God was only putting a comma.

The devil knows my name but calls me by my sin. Jesus knows my sin but calls me by my name.

Seven days without scripture makes one weak.

365 times the bible tells us, 'Do not fear' – that's one for each day.

You cannot kill a spiritually dead person by telling them about Jesus.

God can't steer a parked car (this means God cannot help with your walk if you don't allow Him to be in control), so stay encouraged. Fill your cup with the words from the Holy Bible and be ready to share your love of Jesus for anyone who asks.

The fence – some sit on the fence about God. They deny God for now but reject the devil. They don't understand the devil owns the fence.

T-intersection – walking through life wondering if it's all nonsense. Why follow Jesus? Imagine you come to a t-intersection, a dead end. You're lost and not sure whether to go left or right. You look to the left and see a dead person. You look to the right and see no one. How do you know which way to go? You go right because going left leads to death but the person on the right was resurrected and lives – following Jesus leads to life.

When I read the bible without God in my life, it was too hard to understand and seemed like nonsense but with God in my life, it made sense and had meaning.

Our free will is to either love God or deny God. This can also be simplified as -

To trust God = love God and His will for our lives OR

To trust ourselves = deny God and His will for our lives

I think back to Genesis, specifically, the story of Adam and Eve. This tells us what happens when we love God and trust in God or trust in ourselves. Adam and Eve were created on the sixth day of all creation. They chose to trust in themselves and listen to a deceiver (Satan) instead of their Creator (God) and they were banished from the garden of Eden. They weren't banished because God hated them for doing wrong. Instead, God loved them too much to see them live a life of sin for eternity. God's plan was always for us to have a Redeemer, a Saviour.

In Genesis 3, God tells the snake (serpent who is the devil, Satan) that a male descendant will come from the woman who will bruise the snake's head, but the snake will bruise his heel. That descendant is God's begotten son. Jesus, born through reproduction as a human, as a Savior for all of us.

It all points to Jesus, even from Genesis, God had revealed His plan. His name is Jesus. He alone saves everyone who turns to Him.

> John 3:16 NLT [16] "For this is how God loved the world: He gave his one and only Son, so that everyone who believes in Him will not perish but have eternal life."

> John 14:6 AMP [6] "Jesus said to him, 'I am the [only] Way [to God] and the [real] Truth and the [real] Life; no one comes to the Father but through Me.'"

It's like so many of us who search for God. To try and identify if anything in history noted Jesus was a real person who lived about 2,000 years ago. After reels from my social media about God's love for me started without me searching for them, I wondered if Jesus was real or not. I knew about God, but Jesus, I wasn't so sure about. I found that Genghis Khan had less than 10 manuscripts to prove his existence. Alexander the Great had around 12 manuscripts to prove his existence. Julius Caesar had around 250 manuscripts to prove his existence. I thought about how at school we learnt about most of them through some history classes but during my Catholic school days they did talk about God, I never really knew Jesus was a real person who had lived, died and three days later, was resurrected, but Jesus in history is recorded at least 25,000 times as a real person.

I wondered about forgiveness and heaven, if anyone could believe in God and turn to Jesus themselves to be healed and access heaven. I wondered if that meant people like Hitler could also go to heaven? I found that most people never notice they need a Savior. Who needs a Savior when they don't think they've done anything wrong? Hitler thought he was doing good for everyone by killing millions of people. Hitler never saw that what he was doing was wrong. Much like myself when I was Angry Ange. I never thought I was doing anything wrong either by mistreating others.

We all have moments in our lives when God reveals Himself to us. Sometimes we are ready for it and other times we are not. The bible says Jesus knocks on our hearts to tell us every moment of every day to say He loves us. He wants us to turn to Him so He can heal us of our brokenness and save us, but most don't. Imagine that for a moment. You love family and friends so much, but would you tell them every moment of every day that you love them? Probably not, because telling your children or immediate family every day that you love them seems like enough once a day but not with God. God loves you more than you could ever know, so every moment of every day, He knocks on your heart asking you to turn to Him so He can heal you and save you.

CHAPTER 10

REFLECTION - YOUR WILL FOR YOUR LIFE

Do you even notice your own sinful nature and a need for a Saviour?
Will you let Jesus into your own life?
Will you turn to God and let Him heal you?
Will you choose to love God?
Will you drop your pride and see the benefits of God in your life?
Do you think you had God, but He failed you?
Do you think you had God, but you failed Him?
Do you think you are not worthy?
Do you think you need to get yourself cleaned up before God?
Jesus is the only answer.

John 11:25 AMP Jesus said to her, "I am the resurrection and the life. Whoever believes in (adheres to, trusts in, relies on) Me [as Savior] will live even if he dies;"

These are examples of the free will God has given us. To love God or deny God.

I denied God for decades. Sometimes I felt like God was a business card I held onto, pulling it out when I needed and forgetting about it when I chose my own path, or when life was amazing. My way of doing things before God was only through destruction of relationships with others. Thinking only about what I wanted because I thought it was too hard to love some people. Through my failed religious experiences, I thought God had failed me or I had failed God, not knowing God never fails. Really, I'd never humbled myself enough to allow God into my heart as I still trusted in myself.

I've learnt that the most important choice in this life was to repent of my sins and turn to God. To let Jesus lead my path and direct my way.

Where to from here?

Find a church in your area <u>that's based on biblical truths</u>. Understanding - it's not about rules because in its simplest form God is asking you to choose Him so He can do in your life what He's done in mine and what He's done in so many other millions of Christians', lives. Remember, it's not about a religion, it's about a relationship with God. Pray and ask the Lord to guide you. To bring people into your life who can help you on your own journey. Talk to Jesus, He's a wonderful listener.

Don't forget, we all have a superpower – it's called prayer. Pray from a heart that seeks God.

It's the one thing Satan doesn't want you to do. You seek God and sit to pray and instantly your mind is full of worries. You think to yourself, did I lock the front door? Did I turn the stove off? Did I pay that bill? If you sat and scrolled through social media for hours, you don't have those worried thoughts but the moment you turn to prayer, worries arrive. Remember, those worries aren't from God. Be deliberate and make time for prayer.

> "Dear heavenly Father,
>
> I'm raising up the person who is reading this to you. Lord, please show them the correct path for their lives so

they can understand the love you have for them. You've never asked us to be perfect; you've only asked us to believe in you. Lord, you know everything they've ever done, you know everything they've ever said. You know every thought they've ever had, yet you still love them and ask them to come to you, just as they are.

Jesus, my Jesus, please come into their lives, so they know for themselves that when you return, they are ready.

In Jesus name

AMEN."

CHAPTER 11

TESTIMONIES OF BROKEN PEOPLE IN A BROKEN WORLD

This chapter contains other people in my life who have also found God. They also went from wondering if God was real or totally denying God like I use to do, until they started their own relationships with Jesus.

Be encouraged and I hope that the stories from this book help you make a personal decision on where you choose to take the next step. It doesn't have to be through a religion because for me religion failed me. It's about your own personal relationship with the Lord (Jesus). It's about you choosing God because you notice you need a Savior.

If you're not ready, believe me I get it. I said so many times I had it all sorted too but being Angry Ange, being in control of my life only brought me pain. It didn't take away any of the hurt or the triggers from my childhood or past that I tried to escape until one day God came into my life, and I was reborn - I experienced the new birth. I was no longer angry with the world and though I still haven't read all the bible I don't profess for a moment to know all of it. I'm still a work in progress. I don't even profess to be anything special. All I can do is share my story, the story God wrote for me, so others who have experienced something similar can know for themselves how wonderful it is to invite Jesus into their own lives.

To spend time with others and see their hearts, and to watch for the footsteps of Jesus in other people's lives is amazing. At the very least for you to have a laugh at the old Angry Ange who thought she had it all figured out, never noticing for a moment that I was doing anything wrong until one day I found God was real.

At the end of these testimonies are blank pages for you to write your own personal testimony, to share with your loved one's. None of us can change someones heart to really seek the Lord for themselves but scripture confirms some will sow seeds of Gods truth, others will water it BUT only Jesus can help that seed of truth grow. Always walk with love and kindness because we love our family and friends regardless if they believe or not. Its not about man made rules, its about each person having their own relationship with the Lord.

The Necessity Of The New Birth

From an early age I struggled with anxiety, depression and fitting in. In High School these emotions only amplified and I felt trapped with no way to escape. I questioned lots of things during this developmental stage of my life, but the biggest was - how would I live my life differently if I could start all over again with the life experience I'd gained? It might not be relatable, but I genuinely held onto a hope that someday I would wake up as a baby again! I'd lay awake at night dreaming of the awesome life I could live, but every morning was the same realization - I was still me and I wasn't getting the miracle of a second chance. If only I could somehow get rid of all the mess inside of me and start afresh.

It started to become all too much for me at 16, so I looked for ways to get numbed out. I started to self-harm, I became extremely addicted to pornography, I pushed others away, I pondered suicide and I locked myself in my bedroom playing video games for at least eight hours a day! Anything that made me feel less human was good in my eyes. I'd fight with my Mum and I'd finish every argument by slamming my bedroom door and saying to myself that she was selfish for giving birth to me. That was my way of expressing how I felt, putting the blame on anyone who loved me. All the while hoping that I could somehow have a redo at life. I began to fantasise a lot about running away and starting a new life somewhere else because it gave me a sense of hope that maybe one day things would change.

Suddenly, it's 2020, and I'm in my final year of high school. For probably the first time in my life I wasn't angry about who I was. I was in a committed relationship, I was making money playing video games, I didn't feel anxious, depression was a thing of the past and I had a great friend group. I loved being around my family and I was genuinely thankful for them. But within three months it was all gone. I split up with my girlfriend, I was more anxious than ever, I was back on antidepressants, and I couldn't see my friends because of covid. I started spiralling and I started asking questions again. Why was I born? If I die, can I start again? Is it even possible to have lasting peace? Why do good things never last? All I wanted was to do life all over again so I could get it right.

When I finished school, I became addicted to drugs, alcohol, cigarettes and partying. I shunned my parents, choosing those I'd just met on the street over them. I blamed everything on Mum and Dad, because if it wasn't for them, I never would've been born. I hated everything about the person I was and started processing that through making music! My songs all echoed the same sentiment; I'm a victim, I'm done trying and I hate living. It was around this time that I began to believe that whatever we wanted after death is what we'd receive and I wanted a second go at life and I'd do anything to receive it, because I'd come to the conclusion that nobody on this planet could help fix the mess I'd become.

I wanted change and I wanted freedom, because just smoking weed wasn't cutting it anymore, so I tried harder drugs. I got addicted to Xanax and codeine syrup because they made me forget everything. I gave up on myself even more than before, so I pushed everyone close to me away because they tried to call me out for what I was doing. After a few months of sitting in the back of a car taking all sorts of drugs, I decided it was my turn to drive. I went to a place where they sold drugs with my best friend and bought 20 Xanax tablets. We got in the car and had one Xanax each. This led to five Xanax each and within 10 minutes of leaving the place we had purchased these tablets; the whole bottle of tablets was gone. I blacked out and next thing I know I woke up in a bush shirtless with scratches all over me. Eventually I found my car and I found my friend. My car wasn't drivable. There were alcohol bottles all over the back seat, bong water in the cupholders and a pair of scissors jammed in the ignition! My friend got picked up by some other mates, but I waited alone for my parents to come and save the day. My Dad let me have it on the way home and encouraged me that there was so much more to life than what I had been dedicating myself to!

I laid off the pills and got more into alcohol and weed again. I tried so many times to stop but there was no way I was breaking my habits, I didn't have the strength in myself. My parents suggested so many things, but I didn't want to listen because I resented them for having me.

Eventually, I got singing lessons so my music would sound better and because of these singing lessons my number got passed on to an older guy who wanted to have a chat with me. At this point in time, I'd devoted my life to music because it helped me forget who I was. It was my false hope. On the outside I looked happy, healthy like I actually cared for myself, but everything still lingered below the surface. I was depressed, full of anxiety, addicted to drugs and alcohol and I was in a loveless relationship to get what I wanted.

I arranged a catch up to meet my singing teacher's friend because he offered to buy me coffee and breakfast. I thought he was a lunatic after our first meeting, a drug addict after our second meeting and a man who believed in God after our third meeting, which was all too much for me. He spoke as if he knew God and that God wanted to give me hope, but I didn't want to open my heart again to hope because every time I did it would fail me and I would end up more hopeless than before.

Surprisingly, I started having fights with the girl I was seeing, and I was so frustrated with myself. I tried to take as many drugs as possible, but they didn't help. I tried to self-harm, but it didn't help. I was at my lowest point sitting on a balcony, about 12 floors up and I decided this is it. I'm going to let hopelessness take me into my next life, so I got up onto the railing, looked down and visualized where I'd land. Tears streamed down my face and just as I gained the courage to do it, the girl I was with ripped me down. I didn't understand why she was so angry and upset with me, and I was too hopeless to recognize the trauma of the situation. After smoking some more, I messaged my new-found friend and asked him if we could catch up one morning. He said, "Yes," and we set a time and place for that day.

I got in the car full of guilt, shame, anxiety, anger, and regret. I was a mess and I suddenly remembered something my Mum used to tell me when I was a kid, which was pray to God and He will give you things. So, I started to talk to God, and I let Him have it. I blamed Him for everything in my life and as I did, I remembered a story I'd heard about this transformation that God brings to your life from the inside out when you believe in Him. It flooded my heart and I began to scream at God. Why would He tell me about those things after 20 years of letting me go through so much pain and hurt. If God was really this ever loving, being then He wouldn't have let me suffer under that condition. In a fuel of rage, I screamed and said to God, "God, if you're real, tell me that you have better plans than what I have for myself. If you tell me that I'll serve you for the rest of my life." I felt so smug because there was no way God was going to tell me what I just said in my car. What's He going to do? Part the clouds and let the whole world hear?

I sat down with my friend, still on an emotional rollercoaster. He asked what coffee I wanted, and it felt just like the other conversations we'd had. In my head I was thinking, "Yep, by the end of this chat I'm going to prove that God isn't real because He hasn't answered my request." My friend sat back down and asked me how I was and I was reluctant to answer truthfully. After I gave my quick three-word answer, he looked me dead in the eye and said, "God wants me to tell you something." He then proceeded to tell me exactly what I screamed about to God in the car! I broke down, and I was in complete disbelief. How could he have known? I must've accidentally texted or called him, but I hadn't. He then asked if I felt a knocking on my heart, which I nodded my head to and he said that knocking that I was feeling in my heart, that's Jesus Christ and He wants to move in. Will you let Him? I don't know how many times I said, "Yes," that day.

As the weeks followed, we caught up more and more and I started reading the Gospels and I would weep as I read it. He told me that God wanted me to let go of the drugs, so we organized a day. I had my bong and pipes all in a bag and we prayed that Jesus would take away my drug addiction and I threw it all in the bin. Two weeks later I'd had no withdrawals. He then told me God wanted me to let go of cigarettes and so later that day I went for a walk and prayed that Jesus would take away my cigarette addiction, and I threw them in the bin. Again, two weeks later and I'd had no withdrawals.

Jesus Christ had entered my life and He was quickly moving things around in my heart. I started to pray instead of playing video games; I started to read the bible instead of making music for hours on end and I started journaling about what was happening. That's when I realized, I wasn't depressed, anxious, and filled with guilt or shame; I was completely and utterly free. It was like I was a different person, like I'd been born again. That dream of waking up as a child was becoming a reality.

I tried so many times to beat my addictions, but I never could. I tried to get rid of my depression by seeing a psychologist for years, but it only gave me temporary relief because every night when I was alone it would come back stronger than before. I tried to get rid of my anxiety by telling myself that I had courage, but I couldn't even sit at a cafe for five minutes alone because

I was so sure that everyone was looking at me and judging me for how I looked. I was insecure and I tried to buy the nicest clothes and look the coolest, but every time I looked in the mirror, I felt worthless. It was always me trying to change with no reward. But with Jesus He was effortlessly transforming my life and all I had to do was set my eyes on Him! Within two months everything about my life was different. My desires, what I did in my free time, my associations, my work ethic, and the purest of love had filled my heart and I didn't even have to try. Things that I never thought I could escape were falling off and I was amazed because I knew it had to be God, there was no other answer!

In John 3:6 Jesus says, "That which is born of the flesh is flesh, and that which is born of the Spirit is Spirit." No human being could create the change that happened in my life. That was evident because I tried getting advice from so many people and nothing changed. I had moments where there were glimmers of hope but a week or a month in, it would always come crashing down. John 1:12-13 says, "But to all who did receive Him, who believed in His name, he gave the right to become children of God, who were born, not of blood, nor of the will of the flesh, nor of the will of man, but of God." As I received Him, as I chose Him over this world, and I became born of God. It was that simple.

My life was transformed through one simple decision of saying, "Yes," to Jesus and when I look back at that I realize that's all I need to continually do. I used to hate my Mum more than anyone but once Jesus came into my life, I began to love her again. I began to pray for her and began to hold onto the hope that what Jesus did in me would happen for her as well, because I knew I'd caused immense pain in her heart whilst she watched me suffer all those years. I'll never forget one night we stayed up chatting as we drank hot chocolate and I asked her if there was anyone she hadn't forgiven and she told me all about her life story and that there were lots of people she'd struggled to forgive.

I mustered the courage to say that Jesus can help. And Jesus most certainly has helped; our relationship now is one of love, trust, faith, respect and honour. My Mum is now my best friend, and our relationship is like it was when I was a young child. I adore her as much now as I did back then. That's the life changing power of the new birth: it turns hate into love, offenses into reconciliation and hurt into redemption. The Apostle Paul says in Romans 7:18, "For I know that nothing good dwells in my flesh." The things that dwelt in me were hate, anger, jealousy, depression, anxiety, and strife, these things were killing me. But in its place Jesus brought love, patience, kindness, mercy, peace, a brand-new heart with brand-new desires and a brand-new goal in life. The new birth is the most precious gift in the entire universe because the most precious being, Jesus Christ, bought it for us by being nailed to a cross.

The new birth can't be rightly described by any word, or emotion, or feeling, that's how otherworldly it is. And it's not hard to receive, which is something else I love about it. God made it simple because He loves us so much. I often think about where I would be if I didn't receive this gift and the only answer is that I would probably be dead. I always thought that in this life a second chance wasn't real, but I received the gift of God's immeasurable grace and he continues to pour it out more and more every day.

Getting In The Boat

The old me, two years ago, if we had talked about Christianity or the topic of God, I would have argued long into the night and walked away unable to stop thinking about it. I hated religion and 'overly' religious people. Sure, it was interesting, but I couldn't stand people trying to 'save' me. In fact, I was so bad that at one point early in our marriage, I turned to my husband and said, "If you ever bring religion into our home or family, we're done." I think that might be the textbook definition of a hard heart.

When it came to my views on God, I had a separation from God that felt like a vast chasm that neither of us wanted to cross. I would describe myself as Agnostic and although I thought that I knew a lot on the topic of religion, in actual fact I was misinformed.

My concept of God was along the lines of - I can't be certain He exists or not, so why worry and If He does exist, He certainly isn't involved now, so He couldn't really care that much.

I couldn't deny that there were parts of this world that were far too complicated and wonderful to just be mere coincidence. There simply had to be a designer or Creator in my opinion. Perhaps some of my evidence for this came from my own art and design practices. I know firsthand how difficult it is to create something where all its pieces work together perfectly and how easy it is to make a mistake that messes it all up. Even science seemed to plead the case for a Creator, with everything being too organized. I mean, even the Big Bang theory forces us to ask, "What came before that?" You would think this would have led me directly to the Creator, but I had received many messages throughout my life that religion and Christianity in particular were propaganda of some sort or other, and that the people who followed it were blind fools at best, or unkind and judgmental hypocrites and deceivers at worst.

I also had a very big 'No Good God' problem. If there was a God, he had to be good. No good God would allow so much pain and suffering in the world. No good God would allow his followers to do deceitful or do evil things or to cause pain or suffering in his name. No good God would allow people into heaven if they were mostly good but just happened to not believe in Him or signed onto the wrong religion etc.

Of course, all of this was just me using my little human concept of what was good and bad, to assess the Creator of the universe... rather presumptuous. To me, this meant that our broken world was either entirely humanity's fault because there was no God or it was God's fault for creating broken people. I knew the world was a mess, but I couldn't see the good of religion at all. I was strongly of the opinion that a world without religion where people were just kind to one another would be a better world and that religion should completely be removed from it.

In my personal life, I was in pain and struggling. I put on a good show and to everyone else I had it at least somewhat together, but behind the scenes, I was treading water.

I could see the pain in the world; I had peeled back the curtains of how truly broken our world was. I had come face to face with the evil that was being celebrated in broad daylight and being sold to us as normal and healthy, and I could plainly see that no one who said they had answers actually had any answers. It seemed they were either ill informed, uninformed or serving their own self interests. So, foolishly and unknowingly, I took up the challenge myself. But I could never find a solution to any of the problems, and all that this created in me was an awareness of inferiority about myself, that I also painted everyone else with. I judged others who hadn't come to similar conclusions as me, and judged myself even more harshly, because I thought that's what others were doing.

I was plunged into a continuous cycle of inspiration - hope - extreme responsibility - devastation - hopelessness and despair. Occasionally, on this road to hopeless despair, I would find myself in a place of deep depression and self-hatred. When I hit that place, I thought that perhaps the only answer would be a world without me in it. I was in so much pain, and I was causing so much pain to those around me, every time I went through these spirals of hope and despair, that perhaps the answer was to at least take away as much pain as I could - the pain that I was causing.

As you can imagine, my view of God was not exactly five stars at this point. It seemed to me that we had been left completely alone, with the hardest possible problem, and surely if there was a God, He would have intervened in some huge way to stop our suffering? When you're in darkness like that, it's hard to see the light. In the words of my former self, "If God exists, He must be like a scientist, and we are just a science experiment that He occasionally comes and checks on but can't interfere with because that would ruin the outcomes of the experiment." This was clearly, someone who did not (and at the time could not) understand that God loves us.

It is, I believe, one of the biggest leaps to faith, the concept that God actually loves us. To those who have always believed, that must seem ridiculous, but for those of us on the outside looking in, the concept that someone cares that much for us when we feel abandoned and discarded by ourselves and our fellow humans is challenging. When you have walked alone for so long, and struggled for so long, to hear that someone was walking alongside you the whole time is heartbreaking at first. It is beyond comprehension to hear that someone loves you, knowing all that you know about yourself, that they love all of the secret parts of you, that they love you more than you love you, and that they love you even though you deem yourself unlovable. And if that is true, then what it seems on the surface is that Being who apparently loves you so much couldn't possibly love you at all because they watched your pain and suffering and did nothing to help you. Of course, that's only half the story, but from this perspective it is impossible to see the truth about the love of God.

I started once more on a search for truth. Naively, I thought I had a semi-solid grounding of the truth. We've all been there. But when I had kids, my world flipped on its head. Things that I was so certain of were completely wrong and the proof was staring me in the face, both in the form of these beautiful little lives that I was now responsible for and the life that I was building with my family. I started to seek truth everywhere and to listen to people from all walks of life. That's when things started to shift BUT I was still just a small broken person trying to fix all the broken things I saw in the world and failing because of my own brokenness and lack of understanding. There must be something I was missing. I needed BETTER ANSWERS. TRUER TRUTHS.

My mind became like the walls in a detective's office: red string leading from one idea to the next, to the next and so on. Everything was connected and it was amazing but so complicated and so messy. I started looking for manageable truths, like healthy mind, healthy body things, and found some helpful fixes. But they were small fixes that couldn't come close to fixing all the problems I saw.

Whilst the world continued its descent into darkness despite my best efforts, I also became curious about my Creator, and I was confronted with this simple question one day - If I believed in a Creator, who did I think I was that I shouldn't even try to figure out who He was? No matter how He created me, what method He used, I should at the very least be grateful for all that I have and thank Him. So, I did. I literally said, "I don't know who you are or if you're even listening. You're probably not because I am a tiny human and you would have to be a great and powerful being beyond comprehension and are no doubt extremely busy with all of your powerful being jobs, but I just wanted to say thank you." These conversations continued, and the more I learnt the more I asked. I would get angry at Him sometimes. I asked Him why the world was so messed up, why He did nothing about it, and what tiny humans were supposed to do about it. I became aware that I had done some horrible unspeakable things in my life and was not worthy to be cared for by my Creator, which made me sad, repentant and humble. I thought that if I did not deserve His attention or love for what I had done, at least I knew He could bring forth good things from all of the bad - and my life was evidence enough for that. This brought me into the realization that He did actually care, at least in some capacity. I started to look into which religion spoke of my Creator.

Whilst I was doing this, I was still searching for my own human answers. And then the first domino fell. I came across someone using a verse in the bible to promote an idea my heart knew was wrong. And the verse was this, "Wives submit to your husbands" - that's all he used to promote the idea that the bible supported. That he could have multiple wives and concubines and that they should all do exactly what he said at every moment and have no free will themselves. I thought that if that idea was truly supported in the bible, then at least, I could cross Christianity off as the religion that followed my Creator. But to my amazement it was not, in fact the bible was saying the exact opposite. It asks us first to submit to each other, then the wife to her husband as she would submit to Jesus BUT the requirement for the husband in this exchange is to love his wife, "just as Christ loved the Church and gave Himself up for her to make her holy." According to Christianity, Christ sacrificed Himself for the Church (His people), denied all of his fleshly temptations to serve and protect them and cleanse them of their sins. Now, I thought, that is a husband that I could submit to - someone whose only desire was to provide for and serve their family and deny his own selfish desires. I knew that I could and would submit to someone like that, because I had been blessed with a beautiful husband who already did those things. Instead of the message intended by this online personality, I found the true message from God - one of love and unity. A message of a love so enormous that it was uncomfortable to comprehend. I wondered how many people had misinterpreted, misquoted or twisted scripture to suit their own narratives but more importantly, how many times had I just taken them at their word?

Finally, I asked my Creator, "If you want me to know Jesus, you're going to have to make it pretty clear, I'm not going to seek Him without guidance." Well, as they say, ask and you shall receive. I started to encounter Jesus and Christianity EVERYWHERE. New people whom I met were Christian and no other denominations. I was listening to podcasts about health, fitness, history, social issues, and education - and Christianity would reveal itself, again and again. And I know that some of you might be thinking, that this is just your search algorithms talking, but I promise you, I was not searching for Christianity. I was looking for health and homeschooling information. And, what's more, I had even done more in-depth studies of religion in the past, specifically Christianity, and had come across everything but I hadn't specifically searched about Jesus or love.

But I still had the supernatural claims of the bible to contend with, and to make sure I wasn't being biased, I decided to look into other religions too, using a similar lens. I searched for scientific and historical facts outside of the bible that could support the existence of God, certain events in the bible and in particular the life, death, and resurrection of Jesus. And to my surprise, in my opinion, there was sufficient compelling evidence to support the supernatural claims being made. The more I searched, the more Christianity revealed itself to be true. But for Christianity to be absolutely true, I had to find proof for Christ and the resurrection. History (outside the bible) pointed to Him being a real man who really lived. Other religions regarded Him as important and as a prophet. The world's biggest religion forms the foundation of its belief on one very significant event. But resurrection is quite the claim, and I had to wrestle with the evidence for that. I asked myself this question: What would I die for? My children of course, but would I willingly be crucified for something that I knew to be false? No!!! All except one Apostle suffered a brutal end, for their belief in the resurrection of Jesus Christ. A whole religion spawned almost overnight because there were hundreds of people who had met Jesus, interacted with Jesus, believed that He had resurrected and testified that they had talked, touched and ate meals with Him. People who had persecuted Christians reversed course after an encounter with Jesus after His resurrection. The evidence is out there and there was so much more than I had imagined. But then I had to decide what it all meant and what I was going to do with all of that.

By this stage, I knew I was starting to believe, but I DID NOT WANT TO BELIEVE. To believe would be to go back on everything I had ever said about religion and Christianity and I would look like a fool. But I had to decide if I wanted to look like a fool who had learnt some hard lessons or to actually be a fool given the evidence that I was uncovering. I had to deconstruct my view of Christianity and Christians, to separate religion from religious practices and from believers, and to see Christians for what they truly were. Not people who thought themselves better than others - but works in progress on a journey closer and closer to Christ, working together to carry out God's plan for the whole of humanity. They weren't a bunch of hypocrites as I had previously thought; they weren't foolish for believing supernatural claims. They were just broken humans like the rest of us, trying to fix their problems, but instead of going to broken humans to help, they were taking their problems to their Creator and letting Him help and guide and build them. Jesus was the one holding their hand, so they could walk forward with hope and strength. I had logic-ed my way this far but now came the real struggle. Salvation and Redemption. What was it and why did I need it? What did Jesus really do for me, personally, on the cross?

Imagine you're a pretty good swimmer, you're no Olympic swimmer or anything but you're better than average, and one day, out of the blue, someone hands you a life vest. Well, you probably won't see the need for it, you might even think that person is a little crazy. It's not until you finally realize that what you thought was a swimming pool is actually the middle of the ocean and after hours of treading water and getting nowhere you finally realize that it doesn't matter how good you are at swimming, you desperately need that life vest and you cannot get out of this by yourself.

In a similar way, in the world we tend to assess if we are good or bad people by ranking ourselves based on the actions of others. We keep small tallies in our hearts about what defines us as good or bad. This makes it so easy to define ourselves as good and distance ourselves from all of the wrong that we've done and as a result reject the idea that we deserve punishment for it.

In case metaphors are difficult for you, Jesus and the salvation that He provides is that life vest that I needed but didn't realize when I was first offered it. Nope, first I needed to understand that, contrary to my own belief, I was not as good as I thought. In fact, I was drowning and unable to save myself. I needed that life vest (my salvation offered by the Lord). But I grappled with the question of whether I was willing to accept the free gift of salvation, even though I could see so plainly that by God's standards, and now my own, I both desperately needed it and did not deserve it on my own merit.

I had to realize that no matter what I thought, the gift had already been given, and I couldn't make Him take it back. When I deserved punishment,

He had already said, "No, I have taken this from you, all you have to do is believe and follow me." I was so angry. I thought how is that free-will? Who would I be if I rejected that?

The problem was, I still believed that I deserved what was coming to me... but if that was true, then so did my husband and everyone else I knew... so did my children, and I couldn't bear that. I wanted salvation for my children and my husband and for everyone else in my life. So, why was I so hesitant to accept this vest of life, the free gift of salvation from God for myself? Because I couldn't accept that I was worth that sort of a sacrifice. I had nothing to offer Him. Nothing I could give in return. In my eyes, everyone else was worth this sacrifice, but I was not. And what Jesus was saying was, "No, even you, because I love you, and I want a relationship with you. You are worth the blood that has been paid because I knew you before your mother knew you, I know who you really are now and I know who you will become." And all that He asked from me was that I believed and trusted Him and that I loved Him with all of me. My love in exchange for His. Everything else, God would do or had already done. That was the purest truest version of love that I had ever encountered. I already knew that love was not saving your children from all the pains of this world, love was guiding them through it and using the tribulations to build them up. It was being there and helping them to rise after every fall and loving them, even though they were imperfect. And it was loving them where they were at but wanting better for them because you could see through the image of who they were and who they thought they were, to the image of who they could become.

At the same time, something happened that I can only describe as supernatural. I was grappling with this idea of my sin, salvation and the love of God and how He demonstrates His love, and I could feel that there was still a separation between myself and Him. I couldn't understand what was causing it, because I felt like I wanted to be closer to God to accept the love that He was giving. Was He withholding His presence from me? Well, God showed me, and He gave me exactly what I needed because there was still a part of me that believed that I didn't really need Him. Sure, it would be nice, but I had a pretty great life now as it was and I had done that myself, right? Boy did He show me. Over the course of two days. He withdrew His love and His grace and the connection that I did have with Him and He really humbled me by showing me what I really and truly was without Him. I was depressed, mean and shrouded in darkness. I felt alone and forgotten, and although I was surrounded by family, I felt unloved. I even thought that I deserved this punishment. I was uncertain that I would be able to survive this kind of darkness again, and so I prayed, and when I finally surrendered and asked for help, whilst still questioning if He could or would help, He reached out to me in a vision. He flew me through the universe, through galaxies, through planets, through plants and animals and through my own body, showing me that He was in every cell of my being and in every atom of the universe. He was the reason for it all. He was all powerful and capable of anything. And then He showed me a vision, me standing on a dry riverbed trying to dig my boat out of the sand to gain an inch of ground, instead of waiting for the river to come to me. And the message was clear, "Your way is clearly not working, it never has. It is futile. My way will and I will send the waters but first you have to get in the boat and trust that the waters will come. Sit down and trust in me. Trust that I will provide." I contemplated surrender to let go of my control.

The next day I knew what I had to do. It was still difficult, but I knew that I didn't want a life in darkness without hope and love. He had shown me the fruits of my own life, my personal version of hell, and that His love was the only way out of it. Relinquishing control was a struggle, but I knew now that He knew and loved me as an individual, not just a part of the human race, and that I could trust in His plan for my life because of that. In the same way that I asked my children to trust in me to be there for them every day, I could trust in His plan. After all, He had done a pretty great job with the rest of creation.

So, I got in the boat, so to speak. I surrendered control over everything that I had been trying so hard to control, and gave it back to Jesus. Instantly, like within the hour, my world changed. One minute it was darkness and sadness and desperation and pain and the next I was at peace and hopeful and happy. It was as though someone had lit a blazing torch within me, and it wasn't something that I could have done myself, it was entirely the Lord.

The Rich Man Who Had Much

One of my Dad's favourite quotes was, "Again, I tell you, it is easier for a camel to go through the eye of a needle than for someone who is rich to enter the kingdom of God." (Matt 19:24)

I am that rich man. Growing up, we were by no means wealthy, but we lived in paradise on a little eight-acre property. I had a family who loved and cared for me. By all objective measures, the only way anyone would describe my childhood is idyllic. The oldest of three from a Christian family, I grew up milking cows for pocket money, by hand I might add! Climbed trees that were too high, made swings that were too dangerous, rode motorbikes too fast, and said my prayers every evening. All that is to say, I am in no position to complain about anything in my life! If I tried, it would sound like the moanings of a trust fund baby. Although, if you'd asked me back then to describe waking up early in the morning to trudge through a sometimes shin deep mixture of cow poo, cow wee and mud, then sit down on a tiny stool and squeeze about eight liters of milk out of each of our one to three cows, 'idyllic' would not be the word I would choose.

My parents and grandparents planted the seed of Christ in us at a young age. We said our prayers every night, said grace, and did the occasional bible story, but we never did church. To my understanding, this was because my parents were frustrated with the state of organized religion and failing churches (I think Dad and my pastor would have gotten along!). One thing they were adamant about, though, was the personal relationship with God, directly, not via a proxy like the Pope or some other human being.

I think Mum would have described me as restless as a child and teen. My teachers called it ADHD, but thankfully, Mum and Dad never supported medication. As I moved into my mid to late teens, the rebellion started. I started drinking and smoking pot. By my 20's it was ecstasy, speed, and occasionally cocaine. While working in a London nightclub, we even played a 'game' called floor drugs where the bouncers would just dump the drugs they'd confiscated or found on the floor onto a table and we'd have a bit of a lucky-dip. It was also in my 20's I transitioned from a lanky teen to a pretty good-looking bloke, at least the girls seemed to think so. I was drifting away from the LORD…fast. I think the story of the prodigal son fits me pretty well.

Towards my 20's my restlessness began to mellow, potentially as a side-effect to frying my dopamine receptors. I adopted a 'go with the flow' type attitude and had no real strong convictions. Looking back, this 'go with the flow' was actually abdication. Throughout my life, things just tended to work themselves out, which is a nice way of saying, "Someone else did it". Then, alongside this abdication, I would expect responsibility without actually making any effort to prove deserving or capable of responsibility.

I started to have a very laissez-faire attitude about salvation, something akin to: "Christianity is the easy religion, we're all sinners, we know it, He knows it, Jesus fixed it, see you in heaven, pass me another drink." I would belittle what Jesus did on the cross, make dismissive, disrespectful remarks and crude jokes that I will not repeat here, but for some context. I used to work at a club called Dracula's, my character was Lucifer, and I literally drew up contracts and had people sign their souls over to me for faster drink service.

I frustrated my teachers at school. I had everything going for me, but I just never applied myself. I was utterly disinterested and was generally disruptive; it wasn't until after university that I discovered a love for learning. In saying that, I generally got along with my science and engineering teachers. I have always been into making stuff, so I could see the utility of science and engineering. But flying in those circles I always thought it was incredibly presumptuous when someone would say, "We know God doesn't exist because X." Nothing I've seen comes close to disproving a Creator, sure, maybe not the Christian God, but a Creator of some description. Science itself was created by the church to ponder the wonders of creation. I could talk for days on this topic and it still can get me started at your peril. Just make sure you get a drink and go to the toilet first because you're in it for the long haul.

"Great are the works of the LORD, they are pondered by all who delight in them." (Psalms 111:2) But, no matter how far I drifted, I could never get on board with Atheism. Things are just too organized, too comprehensible, and too fine-tuned to be the result of random processes. I guess I just didn't have enough faith to be an Atheist.

Towards the end of my Dad's life, he was, at least to me at the time, he was getting very pushy when it came to this whole Christian thing. By the time he died, my heart had been hardened so much that all the memories I could recall about Him were negative. I still loved my Dad, but I didn't really respect him. Looking back in hindsight at my Dad, it would seem the apple has not fallen far from the tree.

More recently, in my journey as a father, my priorities were all out of whack. Without a doubt, my kids were (and still are) my responsibility, and I had taken up the responsibility as a father and provider. But OH BOY do those things have a way of highlighting your pride like no other. I have no doubt that's one reason God makes kids the way they are. Frequently, I'll be spending time with them and would have half a mind on work, or some project, or with an eye on the time. I was not there for them 100% in the moment, and they could sense it. When they would inevitably act out, I would get frustrated and angry because they were eating into my time.

So, how did I actually come to Christ after falling away so hard? Well firstly we need to appreciate the 7D chess move God played when He brought my wife into my life. For those of you who don't know, when I met my wife, she was Agnostic at best. On more than one occasion, she told me in no uncertain terms, "If you bring religion into this relationship, we're done!" But it was she who moved first. If we had met any earlier in life, during my party phase then she wouldn't have touched me with a 10-foot pole. On the flip side, If I had been zealous for the LORD when we met, she would have run for the hills. As an aside, a day or so after we met, I was taking the night bus back from working at a bar when who should get on the same bus but my future wife. Turns out we were on the same bus route. When I told the guys from work about this, one of them said, "Haha, well that's God just saying, "There you go mate!"

We would talk about the broken world and the incremental but noticeable degradation of values and morals. Though when reflecting on the life of my past self. I recalled that for me, there always seemed to be hard lines I would not cross. It was like God had earmarked my heart, and this somehow held me back. I began to appreciate that things 'just working out' may have an explanation in Christ. Because, if I'm honest, it's by the grace of God alone that I did not end up in prison, dead in a car crash, or in a ditch. It's by the grace of God that I was not in the cubicle when nightclub security kicked the door in. It's by the grace of God that I was not with my best mate through high school and university when he went off the rails and got hit by a truck; we're still not sure if it was deliberate. It's by the grace of God I've walked away from multiple DUI car crashes. It's by the grace of God that I didn't totally cook my brain after years of partying so hard that even my friend had to tell me to slow down. I could keep going, but you get the picture.

I have no doubt that the upbringing and the faith of my mother and father, grandparents and great-grandparents all played a supernatural part in me standing here today. The book of Acts says, "Believe in the LORD Jesus, and you will be saved, you and your household." And Matthew and

Mark both quote Deuteronomy, "These commandments that I give you today are to be on your hearts. Impress them on your children. Talk about them when you sit at home and when you walk along the road, when you lie down and when you get up."

Given my upbringing, a particular hurdle I had to overcome was whether I believed what I believed because I was indoctrinated as a child or because I had come to it of my own volition. I had drifted to the point of thinking maybe the bible was 2000 years of Chinese whispers. And that God punishing us for not believing in some guy supposedly being crucified 2000 years ago seems a bit petty (I actually said that to my Christian father). Now, though with this wonderful woman in my life who was now my wife on the Jesus train and religion no longer off limits, and with a soft heart, I started listening to preachers like John Bevere, and Mike Welles, and the YouTuber Inspiring Philosophy, but most importantly, I began to actually consume The New Testament and found it was just truth bomb after truth bomb. It so accurately described the world and its problems. I even discovered there is non-biblical evidence for Jesus and compelling arguments for the resurrection.

When my Mum asked me how I felt about my wife coming to Jesus, I said, "Relieved." It wasn't like I'd been a closet Christian, secretly waiting for this moment, but when she came to Christ, and I saw the rapid and effortless positive changes she experienced, it softened my heart to the LORD, and I began to seek, so eventually, I found.

Along with relief, I also felt like a bit of a coward, that if I had been strong in my convictions and pursued Jesus earlier rather than push Him aside, then maybe my now wife, may have seen the fruits of my Christian walk and jumped on the Jesus train sooner. For as my pastor says, "For the unbelieving husband has been sanctified through his wife, and the unbelieving wife has been sanctified through her believing husband. Otherwise, your children would be unclean, but as it is, they are holy." (1 Cor 7:14) But, as we know, He works all things together for good for those who love the LORD (Rom 8:28).

Another challenge was my pride. I didn't think I was particularly proud, after all, I didn't have any real strong convictions, how could I be prideful? Well, didn't the LORD have a bellringer of a lesson for me? I was at the Broadwater with the kids and the dogs, my wife was home, and I was swimming with the kids. There was a guy on his phone, not controlling his dog, and it kept running over and barking at my two dogs. It was not aggressive, it just would not stop, and this bloke could see what was going on but couldn't be bothered to pause his call and call his dog back. Eventually, I called out, and he did something about it. I would never let my dog do that! I thought. What an inconsiderate, naughty word of a person! I was so annoyed! While I was stewing there in my anger, I faintly heard my four-year-old son say, "What are you doing you silly-billy?" I turn around, and he is cradling my daughter and she's crying and coughing up water. She had lost her balance in two feet of water and had gone under and my AMAZING SON had snatched her from drowning. I was so caught up in my self-righteous pride and anger, thinking how annoying this bloke was for allowing his dog to misbehave, that my 18-month-old daughter almost drowned less than two meters away from me. Praise the LORD that my son was there and by God's endless grace, He kept her safe, because I failed her that day in a way words cannot describe, all because a dog was barking!

And I remember the moment when I actually made the conscious decision to say, "I'm in," I was mowing the lawn and listening to the book of Matthew, and He was just dropping truth bombs! I was shouting, "Yesss, Amen!" in my backyard. Then it got to the parable of the seeds: "A farmer went out to sow his seed. As he was scattering the seed, some fell along the path, and the birds came and ate it up. Some fell on rocky places, where it did not have much soil. It sprang up quickly, because the soil was shallow. But when the sun came up, the plants were scorched, and they withered because they had no roots. Other seeds fell among thorns, which grew up and choked the plants. Still other seeds fell on good soil, where it produced a crop-a hundred, sixty or thirty times what was sown. Whoever has ears, let them hear." (Mat 13 3-9).

After I heard this, I said to myself, I know what seed I want to be! I stopped mowing and said out loud, "I'M IN! LET'S DO THIS." I began to list off and repent for all the horrendous things I'd done to disrespect what He'd done for me. It was like a wall around my heart had finally fallen, and his love could come in. I realized I NEED HIM! I wanted to do His will; I wanted to want what He wanted. I wanted to let Him drive; I wanted to let Him change me from the inside.

After that day, things shifted in my heart. I really want to hammer home that this was not me simply following a bunch of rules that had been imposed on me. I'm still doing the things I want to do, it's just that those things are different. Rather than pursuing selfish career goals, I want to build community and disciple my kids. Instead of wanting to watch streaming services, I'm excited to go to church. I used to listen to some pretty full-on psytrance music, but now I praise music that cuts straight to my heart! I am filled with gratitude for everything in my life, gratitude for things that I do not deserve but through His grace have been given to me.

Another thing I want to hammer home is that I'm not perfect (shock-horror-gasp!), no one is. Sometimes I lose my temper and a swear word pops out, sometimes I'll get sucked down a YouTube rabbit hole when I should be reading the bible, but it's different now. When I slip up, I feel like I've disappointed someone I love and respect ... because I have. My pastor says it best, "Therefore, if anyone is in Christ, the new creation has come: The old has gone, the new is here!" (2Cor5:17).

My priorities have totally shifted when I spend time with the kids instead of having one eye on a project or something. I am all in for them, not only as a provider and protector but as a priest and leader. When it's clock-off time, that's it. The computer is off and I'm with them 100%. It's not biblical, but it is apt. The only people who will remember you working nights and weekends are your children, or no child ever said, "Gee, I wish parents worked more!" I'm not trying to get all high and mighty here, I am in a very fortunate position where my job doesn't require me to be away at all, and my income can support our family, but it's not without sacrifice. A second income would afford us many nice things, but this is the choice we made. I respect my Dad for being there in my life, coaching my basketball teams, and disciplining me in his own way.

With this also came a calmer nature towards the inevitable challenges that kids and family life brings. This is going to sound a bit contradictory but stay with me. Before, I was a chilled-out guy, but this chill was almost out of spite or prideful defiance to the stressors around me. When my wife would get stressed, my pride in my calm nature would reinforce my resolve to remain calm. It wasn't until now (writing this testimony) that I could actually put words to it. No wonder it used to drive my wife up the wall! Now, I'm still a pretty calm bloke, but not to the point of abdication. Also, my relaxed nature now has its foundation built on the solid rock of the LORD rather than the sand of: *Things just seem to work themselves out"*.

I have become more intentional, both in my personal and professional life. As a leader, my priority is to serve Christ and in order to serve Christ, I must serve my family and the church, not be served by them. A good leader eats last. As the strong man, you show your strength in restraint, not in force. All of this is to crucify my pride every day. I recently had a dream where I was told to "dissolve into the church". I don't think there's a better way to describe sacrificing my pride than to dissolve like salt into water.

I've become more intuitive when it comes to my relationships. To be fair, any intuition would be better than essentially zero. Little things like putting a hand towel back nicely, but also seeking out responsibility at work and being proactive, not reactive, when it comes to my relationships. My relationship with my wife and our kids has never been closer. That's not to say we were dysfunctional beforehand. By worldly measures, we were doing pretty well, but now I feel like we're so much more connected. We're thriving as a family walking with the LORD. We still have our challenging times personally, financially, or otherwise, but now we're grounded in a deep, abiding trust in the LORD.

Again, I really need to stress this, particularly to those not in the faith. ALL of this change has come from the simple act of earnestly relinquishing my prideful grip on my own life and allowing my maker to guide me. Trusting that, although you cannot tell where the wind comes from or where it is going, it will deliver you to exactly where He needs you to be.

One thing I didn't really know how to thread into this was the lies that are incepted into your mind by the world and/or the enemy. Before coming to Christ, I would get these nit-picky thoughts whenever the topic of Jesus or Christianity would come up. I didn't think much of them until after I said, "I'm in." Then, like a flood, for about a month or so, they were coming in hard and fast, but one instance stood out more than any other. I walked into church, and on the board was something akin to: "The greatest thought God had when He created the universe was His Church." It honestly felt like something hit me in the head. And the lie was: Seems a bit selfish, la di da. Create an entire universe just so He can be worshipped!

I could tell immediately that this was not my own thought. This came from elsewhere; it was like the enemy had shown his hand, and now I was onto Him.

Sure, the church worships God, but it's much, MUCH more than that. We are made in the image of God, as His ambassadors in this life, and He created us so we can have a personal relationship with Him. He has a purpose for us we can't begin to imagine. Get this! Paul says in 1 Cor 6:3, "Do you not know that we will judge angels?" WHAT!!!

Finally, one more and we'll get on with burying the spiritually dead man through my water baptism. This lie was:

Imagine a relationship where the more powerful member says, "Stay with me, or else bad things will happen." By any measure this seems like an abusive relationship. Then isn't our relationship with God an abusive one?

The resolution to this was shown to me in such a beautiful way. I was in the pool holding my daughter, and true to her nature, she wanted to do it herself. She was struggling and squirming and saying, "I can do it myself!"

I obviously love my daughter very much, so I say to her, "You need to stay with me, if I don't hold you, you will die." This is clearly not an abusive relationship. I even let her have it her way and let her go, unsurprisingly, she sinks, and I pull her back up, tell her I love her, and give her a cuddle. After regaining her composure, she remains calm for a little while, then, after she rebuilds some confidence, continues to carry on wriggling. This is what a relationship with God is like. We have the wriggly, squirmy children saying, "I can do it myself." And God is the loving father who will hold us and guide us, but who loves us enough to let us sink for a bit if we get a bit too big for our britches.

> "A fool spurns a parent's instruction, but whoever heeds correction shows prudence." (Prov 15:5)

Many men grapple with The Fear of the LORD, but the women do too, but, at least in my limited experience, the men seem to focus on it more. This verse from Luke really hit home for me. Luke 12:48 (quoting Jesus Himself) "From everyone who has been given much, much will be demanded; and from the one who has been entrusted with much, much more will be asked."

I have much...we all have much.

The Friend Who Gave His Life For Me

I was brought up through my childhood, emotionally and verbally abused. Simple things like asking what is for dinner would result in getting screamed at and told I'm not doing enough and that I am ungrateful. Though I never knew my parents while they were together, when they would drop me off it would often turn into a screaming match. Occasionally, I thought a fist-fight was going to break out between my stepdad and my Dad.

The trauma and pain built up, and from the age of eight I would close myself in the bathroom and cry to myself. I didn't know why but I felt like I was living under a big black cloud, it was the trauma of my upbringing. I spent every moment I could gaming, living in a different world, hours before and after school, it often felt like my only safe haven.

I got expelled from high school when I was 12 years old for selling marijuana, trying to be like my parents and role models, who were selling and smoking drugs and telling me stories of their 'glory days' partying and doing lots of drugs. At this point I realized where I was headed, to an angry lonely existence like those who raised me. I needed to do something different; I didn't want to be like them. I swore off ever doing alcohol or drugs and vowed to end up different than those who were raising me. But I still went home and had to deal with the same abuse and neglect. The pain continued to build up. I felt like my past was so heavy and I had to try and distance myself from it. I would play games, watch pornography to try to escape and give myself a moment of distraction. Then I started lifting weights at 15 and I got obsessed with it. I didn't understand why, but at the time I thought that it would make me valuable or feel like somebody if I got big and strong enough. I spent more and more time lifting weights; my whole life was structured around how I could get stronger. I would train so hard that I would have spots all over my skin from where I'd gotten my blood pressure so high that I burst blood vessels. On top of that I bulged a disc in my back and continued to squat 150kg through the pain - the things I did to try to make myself feel better.

It wasn't making me feel any better, I still felt worthless, and lonely. Battling my past. But it provided me enough of a distraction that I was getting by. I got a job using my university degree and I thought I was on my way to being different from my parents, like I had it figured out. I would work and get enough money and then I would be happy and my past would no longer affect me.

I was still training hard, still trying to find escapes from life but now I had work and a career to distract me as well. Then my Dad got diagnosed with cancer and I was his primary carer. I would take him to hospital and sit with him and be the one who had to remember every doctor's appointment, spend days and days sitting in the cancer ward of the hospital and be the one responsible for his life and death medical decisions when, due to sickness, he was unconscious or not in a good state of mind. I was still training, still lifting weights while looking after my Dad. When he passed away, I was crushed, and I began to go through bouts of serious depression. I would be reliving and ruminating about all the horrible things that had happened. I couldn't get away from it. No amount of training or work or money would cure me or distract me. My past was so heavy.

I continued for a year feeling like I was drowning. I would get some relief for a week or two before being pulled down for another two weeks, and waking up having panic attacks literally every night. My coping mechanisms weren't working and I was lost.

Then, by chance, I took singing lessons, and after talking about my life a little bit my singing teacher gave me the number of a man. I was so hopeless that I would talk to anyone, so I went out for a coffee with him. He had a similar past saying that his father had passed away early and he had a traumatic rough upbringing. But he managed to let go of it all and find true peace. He started telling me about the new birth, that by fully accepting in his heart the sacrifice Jesus had made for him, He had received a new life and felt peace for the first time.

I was fascinated; no one had given me a story like that before. I had nothing to lose. I began meeting with this man trying to understand how to get this same peace. I went all in, trying to give my heart to Jesus. About two weeks of obsessing over this, I was reading the Gospel of Matthew, Jesus is on the cross, and while reading about all he went through I started crying. I realized how much He gave up, how much He went through for me, how much He loves me to do that. I realized that if a friend gave his life for me, I would be so indebted to him. I would do anything he asked. How could I not give my life for Jesus? That afternoon I felt the most peculiar sense of peace.

The weeks went on and the panic attacks stopped, and the rumination about past traumatic events stopped as well. I lost the obsession with the things I was doing to distract myself. I could do them for their own sake rather than to make myself feel worth something or to distract myself from the state of pain I was in. It felt like the cord had been severed from my past.

Truly, all the pain from my past was taken from me and placed onto Jesus and I got a new life, like I had been born anew and given a fresh start. As the months have gone on this feeling hasn't gotten old. There are times when thoughts about past horrible events pop up, but they are devoid of any emotion, they don't pull me into depression or anxiety, they just pop up and pass away. I had been running and running from my past, trying to distract myself and I thank God every day for giving me a way out, the only way out. And for putting someone into my life who had experienced that and shared their miracle of the new birth with me. The best thing I ever did was take that person seriously and chase Jesus with all my heart.

Shame Turned To Innocence

Growing up, I had a lot of insecurities regarding how I felt in comparison to others. Being the youngest of four, I was trapped in what felt like an uncontrollable comparison. I would find any means to belittle myself, always seeing others as better than I was, like I was always inadequate.

Through my teen years I started to do more to fit in, because this seemed like the only way that I might start to feel adequate. But over time, my actions only drew me further from who I was, and as a result I was the furthest I had ever been from happiness. I was perpetually depressed, I struggled to feel anything, and I resorted to self-harm as a means to overcome the numbness I felt.

This went on for some time, until I started to find things in the world that got me recognized. My soccer started to become a source of recognition, so I thought the world could see me, but it turns out, I didn't care about people seeing me, I just desired to feel something, to feel anything. That's exactly what overtraining was doing. It was truly just another means of torturing my own body. A torture worth all the shame I felt. The shame of being worthless.

I had a massive void that I couldn't fill alone. And no person on this earth could fill that void either.

Now, up until this point in my life I had never had any interest in God, and any mention of anything spiritual would have me turn up my nose and walk away. I didn't believe in anything after death, just simply that we live and then die… nothing more.

But at this point, too many things started to happen that couldn't simply be explained as a coincidence.

I had a pretty serious sports injury, stunting my ability to overtrain. One week before my injury my boyfriend's Dad was diagnosed with cancer.

Four months later, my boyfriend's Dad passed away. Five months later I had another sports injury, which resulted in me being in a moonboot for three months.

I had a realization that there was indeed something missing from my life. I wanted to do something with my life, and I definitely didn't want to just live and then die.

I left my job with nothing else planned, but rather the idea that I needed to change everything in my life if I was to change my trajectory and find my true purpose. Three weeks after I left my job, my boyfriend told me we were invited over for dinner at some Christian's house. I was unsure at first, but I wanted to support his curiosities, so I went along, purely as his girlfriend, with no interest in understanding their beliefs.

But this is when my life flipped the right way round.

They were so welcoming and friendly. They made us feel like we were home. We stayed for hours and they never complained once. It was the most enjoyable conversation I had ever had. They were so whole, and we wanted what they had. They invited me back to a lady's group they ran from their home every week and I went along, figuring I had all the time and nothing to lose. The ladies there were so friendly and gave the sweetest of hugs. They shared their testimonies and I started to relate to some of the things they were sharing. And my hard heart started to soften towards God. I started to see that God is real! I could see that the certain order of events in my life, especially in the past couple of years, were no coincidence. The only answer was that they were crafted by our very own Creator. I wanted what these ladies had, and I was hungry to know more. God was drawing me in and He was drawing me into a community that wanted to accept me as myself.

Since the day I accepted the Lord into my heart I have seen so much growth and endless peace. The depression and anxiety are all gone. I know that truly anything is possible with Jesus and that there is nothing that we need to worry about. I am no longer worthless, but rather have the ultimate purpose of serving God.

Having Jesus in my life has been an absolute game changer.

I had been in a relationship for over eight years, but it was starting to feel more like a convenience and was getting rather stagnant. Now, in just four months with the Lord, we have the healthiest relationship we have ever had. My now husband also found Jesus at the same time as I did. We decided to stop living in sin. We needed to 'flee from temptation', so I moved out and three days later we got engaged. Our relationship felt like it had a high school innocence to it, and we really started to grow in the Lord as individuals, ready to start our marriage from a place of purity with foundations from the Lord. God stripped our broken views on marriage, and is teaching us his holy ways, in the hope of having a holy family in His image.

We are now happily married and we are so grateful for the time we had living apart before stepping into this season of marriage. Things that felt shameful before, now feel beautiful and innocent. I thank the Lord for that every day! He has a true and intended purpose for everything.

This is just four months of growth with the Lord. I can't wait to see what a lifetime with the Lord looks like.

My Heart Searched For Truth

I have believed in God for as long as I can remember. Even as a child, before I had words to explain it, my heart knew there was something greater than me. Deep inside, I also knew something else that was harder to accept: I knew I was not a good person, and I knew I needed a Savior. That awareness was not born out of fear, but out of an inner conviction that I could not carry life on my own. Yet, despite this belief, I did not truly know God, and I certainly did not know how to love Him.

The cross, in particular, felt strange and uncomfortable to me. I could not understand why suffering, blood, and sacrifice were central to faith. It felt distant and abstract, almost unsettling. I believed God existed, but I did not grasp His love, His holiness, or the depth of what Jesus had done. God was real to me, but He was not close.

I grew up in an Atheist and dysfunctional family, where faith was neither taught nor encouraged. There was little emotional stability, little sense of safety, and no spiritual foundation. As a result, I learned early on to survive on my own. I became independent in unhealthy ways, believing that strength meant self-reliance and that asking for help was weakness. I carried wounds I did not know how to name, and emptiness I did not know how to fill.

As a teenager, that emptiness grew louder. I began using drugs and constantly seeking validation from people. I wanted to be seen, loved, chosen, and approved of. My worth depended on the opinions of others, and I shaped myself to fit whatever I thought would earn their acceptance. Inside, however, I felt deeply lost. My heart was empty, restless, and hopeless. I was surrounded by people, yet profoundly alone. I tried to silence the pain with distractions, but nothing lasted. No matter what I did, there was a void that refused to be filled.

In my twenties, something shifted. The noise of my lifestyle could no longer drown out the quiet longing in my heart. I found myself yearning to know God—not just to believe in Him, but to understand Him. I had so many questions about life, suffering, identity, and purpose, and I slowly began to realize that God was the only possible answer to all my questions. At the same time, I was still living as if life was all about me. I could not see beyond my own needs, desires, and wounds, and I did not yet understand that I was not the centre of the world.

God, in His mercy, began to lead me gently but firmly. He brought me to another country, far from everything familiar. I did not know it at the time, but this displacement was part of his plan. Away from my old environment, my old habits, and my old identity, He placed a deep conviction in my heart: I needed to surrender my life to Him. Not partially. Not conditionally but completely.

I had reached the end of myself. I had tried for years to change on my own—to fix my behavior, control my emotions, and become someone better through my own strength. But nothing worked. The cycle of despair, self-effort, failure, and shame kept repeating. Eventually, I had to hit rock bottom. And there, with nothing left to rely on, I finally asked for help. I stopped trying to save myself and admitted the truth: I could not do it.

That moment of surrender changed everything. I told God, with honesty and humility, "I can't do this, but you can." God did not reject me. He did not rush me. He had been patiently waiting for me all along. He met me exactly where I was, not with condemnation, but with grace. Slowly, faithfully, He began to set me free from the patterns that had imprisoned me for so long.

God transformed me from the inside out. He gave me a new identity in Christ—one that was not based on my past, my mistakes, or others' opinions, but on His truth. Although I still remember my past, and although it can be painful at times, it no longer defines me. God placed people in my path who helped me heal, who spoke truth over me, and who walked with me as I learned who I was in Him. Through them, Jesus restored what had been broken and rebuilt what had been lost.

My relationship with God continues to deepen every day. Faith is no longer just something I believe—it is someone I walk with. God is no longer distant or abstract; he is present, personal, and faithful. I am learning daily what it means to trust Him, obey Him, and love Him, even when I do not fully understand His ways.

If I had to make my decision again, I would choose Jesus every single time. I would give Him my life again and again, every day. Because true freedom did not come from fixing myself—it came from surrendering to the One who already paid the price for me. And in Jesus Christ, I finally found what my heart had been searching for all along.

Your testimony

Your testimony

Your testimony

Your testimony

www.ingramcontent.com/pod-product-compliance
Lightning Source LLC
LaVergne TN
LVHW090934080826
845145LV00003B/750

* 9 7 8 1 7 6 4 5 6 2 0 6 5 *